101
TRADITIONAL
CHRISTMAS
GIFTS

101
TRADITIONAL CHRISTMAS GIFTS

LIZ STUCKEY

with charts and illustrations by the author

David & Charles

This book is dedicated to the memory of my sister Tricia,
who had every confidence in my ability, and to my
husband Carsten, for his unceasing support.

A DAVID & CHARLES BOOK

First published 1992
First published in paperback 2003

Distributed in North America by
F&W Publications Inc
4700 East Galbraith Road
Cincinnati, OH 45236
1-800-289-0963

A catalogue record for this book is available from the British Library.

ISBN 07153 1576 5

Typeset by ICON, Exeter
Printed in Great Britain by Butler & Tanner Ltd
for David & Charles
Brunel House Newton Abbot Devon

Designed by COOPER WILSON DESIGN, London
Photography by Belinda Banks and Amanda Cooke

CONTENTS

INTRODUCTION

Christmas won't be Christmas
without any presents
Louisa May Alcott – Little Women, 1868

When the chilling frosts and snows of winter cast a cloak across the land, our thoughts are warmed by the prospect of the final celebration of the year. Christmas is the time when families get together to exchange presents, and goodwill is matched by the feasting and frivolity of the season. We all have our childhood memories of Yuletide, with many traditions handed on by our parents, grandparents, family and friends; yet however hard we may try to preserve these ideals we are being constantly bombarded by commercialism, encouraging us to spend, spend, spend. But if we stand back for a moment and take stock of ourselves, we find that many creative ideas and the gifts that flow from them are well within our own capabilities; and that we may be saving money into the bargain.

The aim of this book is to encourage young and old alike to join in preparing for a traditional Christmas. If you follow the instructions closely you will be amazed at what you can achieve. There is as much pleasure in the making of presents as in the receiving, and the personal touch adds an extra dimension to anything from the shops. In the following chapters there lies a treasure trove of ideas, including floral decorations, tree ornaments, festive food, table decorations, gifts for family and friends and a wide range of other suggestions.

The materials used throughout this book are readily available from garden centres, florists and craft shops, or by mail order from Fred Aldous Ltd (PO Box 135, 37 Lever Street, Manchester M60 1UX), but many can be obtained for free. When you are out walking during the year, keep an eye open for interesting materials which could be adapted for decoration: branches, cones and seed pods, for instance, all have their place. As summer turns to autumn, gather suitable flowers and foliage for drying. Collect boxes and cartons, for these can be transformed into excellent gift packages.

Begin your Christmas planning now, and benefit from the 101 exciting ideas in this book. You will find many will make excellent gifts for other occasions, too. Happy Christmas!

CHAPTER ONE

DECORATING THE HOME

FRONT-DOOR WELCOME GARLAND

What better way to greet your friends than with this cheerful garland? It will impart the true Christmas spirit on your doorstep.

MATERIALS

1 straw or foam ring 30cm (12in) in diameter
Sprigs of evergreen such as blue pine
Dried lichen moss
1m (40in) red satin ribbon 10cm (4in) wide
Glue
Florist's wire and scissors
Decorations: artificial sprays, apples, nuts, cones etc

Break up 5cm (2in) clusters of moss and fix to the ring by wrapping fine wire in and out of it, then twist the ends of the wire together to secure, or glue the moss with a strong adhesive. Wrap fine wire around a sprig of evergreen and attach to the ring over the moss, bending the wire over and under securely. Work around the ring, covering the ends of the previously attached sprig with a new one. Wire or glue the other decorations to the ring to give a balanced arrangement.

Insert a 5cm (2in) piece of wire into the top of the ring on the reverse side and twist the ends together to make a hanging loop. Twist some wire through the back of the bow and attach to the top centre front of the garland to complete.

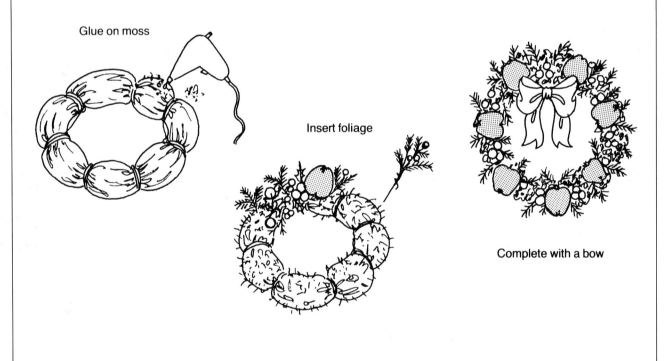

Glue on moss

Insert foliage

Complete with a bow

Holly Kristtorn, the word for holly in Danish and Swedish, translates as 'Christ's thorn' so named because it was thought that drops of Christ's blood spilled by the crown of thorns coloured the berries red.

FIREPLACE SWAG

*I*f *you have a fireplace, make this festive decoration to embellish it and give a focal point to your room at Christmas. The swag could also be used to decorate the handrail on a staircase.*

MATERIALS

Sprigs of evergreen such as blue pine, dried lichen, moss
Florist's wire and cutters
2 x 1m (40in) lengths of cord with tassels
Straw plait 1m (40in) long
Wide brown adhesive sealing tape
Wide ribbon or florist's crinkle paper for bow
Decorations: bought trims, nuts, cones, gold and red baubles etc
2 candle-holders and candles

Stair-rail Swag
Spiral a narrow piece of mixed gold and red tinsel around a wider piece of pine green tinsel, and use to wrap around banisters or stair rails for a simple but striking effect.

Wrap the moss around the plait and secure it by twisting wire in and around the moss and the plait. Attach lengths of tasselled cord to each end of the plait with wire: thread the wire through the cord and the straw, and twist the ends of the wire together to secure.

Beginning at one end of the moss-covered plait, attach a sprig of evergreen with wire, then add more sprigs, each overlapping the ends of the last one. Work down the length of the plait in the same way. Wire up the trim decorations by twisting wire around stalks and cones. To wire nuts, make a small hole with a skewer, insert wire and add a dab of glue where wire meets shell. Insert trim decorations at evenly spaced intervals.

Fasten the swag to the mantelpiece over the fireplace with some of the adhesive tape in the centre and at each end. Allow the tasselled ends of the swag to hang down at each side. Attach a large bow to the middle with a piece of wire, then attach candle-holders at each side and insert candles.

Insert foliage and trims into plait

Fix tasselled cord to plait

Finished swag with candles

SAFETY FIRST *Do not allow candles to burn too low, or leave lit in an unoccupied room.*

▶ *Fireplace Swag; Giant Machine-Knit Stocking; Velvet and Needlepoint Stocking*

SANTA'S KNIT STOCKING

*K*nit this jolly stocking with its seasonal motifs to hang at your children's bedside. Watch their faces light up when they wake up to find it filled with goodies. If you are more ambitious, you can make a pair to snuggle up in by the fireside awaiting Santa's arrival!

MATERIALS

For medium size lady's foot:
50g (2oz) ball royal blue double knit yarn
50g (2oz) ball red double knit yarn
25g (1oz) ball brown double knit yarn
25g (1oz) ball white double knit yarn
Oddments of double knit yarn in gold, black, flesh
Set of four 4mm (UK 8, USA 6) double-ended knitting needles
(Yarn quantity is enough for a pair)
(For knitting terms and methods see Techniques.)
Tension: 24 stitches and 27 rows to 10cm (4in) on 4mm (UK 8, USA 6) needles in st st.

Cast on 52 st in red yarn, equally spaced over three needles. Work 20 rounds in K1, P1, rib.

Continue working from Chart A in stocking stitch, starting from the top right of the chart, joining in colours as required. Pattern repeat is worked 4 times for the snowflake and reindeer and 5 times for the hearts.

When the 64 rows from Chart A have been worked, join in the royal blue yarn and work 1 round, decreasing 1 st at the end (total 51 sts, leg length 30cm (12in) approx).

HEEL SHAPING

Next round: K13, turn, P24, turn.
Working on two needles, knit 20 rows in st st across the 24 sts.
Row 1: Turn, K16, sl 1, K1, psso.
Row 2: *Turn, sl 1 purlwise, P8, P2 together.
Row 3: Turn, sl 1 knitwise, K8, sl 1, K 1, psso.*

Repeat from * to * until 10 sts remain. Continue knitting on four needles in rows.
Next row: K10, K up 11 sts from side extension of heel, K27, K up 11 sts from other side of heel (total 59 sts).
Work the pattern from Chart B, joining in colours as required.
Next row: K22, K first row from chart across following 25 sts, inc 1, turn.
Next row: P1, P second row of chart, P remaining 34 sts inc 1 st at end, turn. (Total 61 sts)
Next row: K1, sl 1, K1, psso, K30, K2 tog, K third row from chart, K1, turn. (Total 59 sts)
Next row: P1, P fourth row from chart, P33, turn.
Next row: K1, sl 1, K1, psso, K28, K2 tog, K fifth row from chart, K1, turn. (Total 57 sts)
Next row: P1, P sixth row from chart, P31, turn.
Continue in this way, shaping the heel and following the chart until 51 sts remain. Continue remaining rows without shaping until all pattern rows have been completed.
Next row: join in red yarn, sl 1, K1, psso, K to last 2 sts, K2 tog. (Total 49 sts)
Continue working in rounds until foot measures 20cm (8in).
Working with 3 needles, divide the stitches up thus: first and second needle 12 sts, third needle 25 sts, and work the toe, shaping as follows.

TOE CAP

Round: First needle: sl 1, K1, psso, K to end. Second needle: K to last 2 sts, K2 tog. Third needle: sl 1, K1, psso, K to last 2 sts, K2 tog. Repeat this round until 17 sts remain. Break off yarn, leaving enough to use for grafting the toe together. Graft toe, secure yarn.

MAKING UP

Sew in loose ends. Following the maker's instructions for pressing, press the stocking. Join foot seams and back seam with small backstitches.

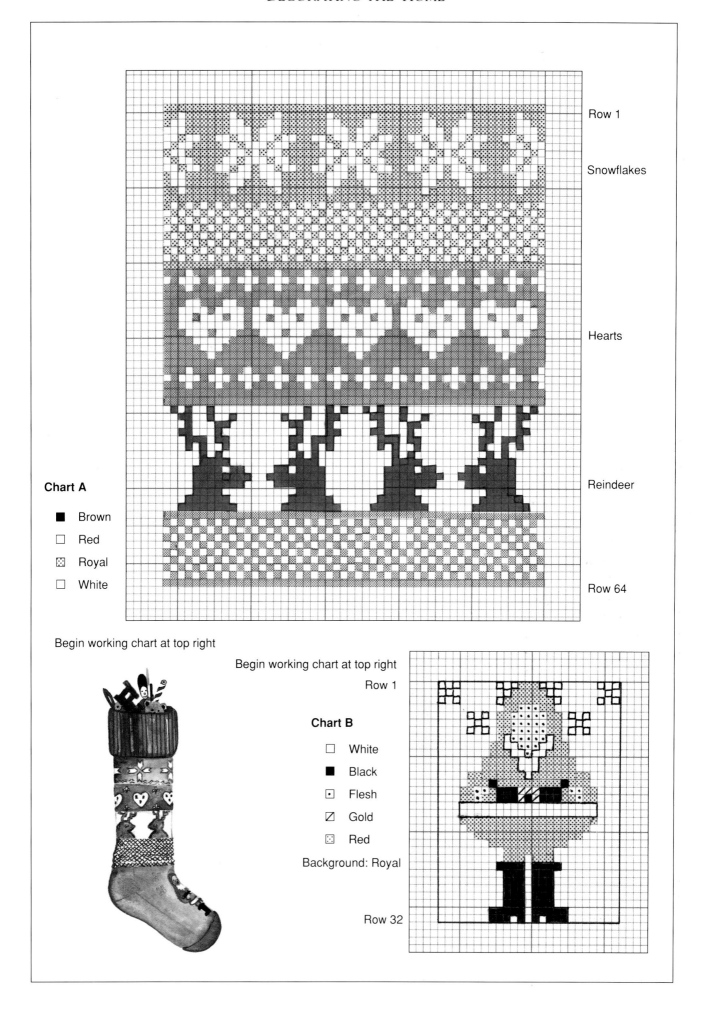

Row 1

Snowflakes

Hearts

Reindeer

Chart A

■ Brown
□ Red
▣ Royal
□ White

Row 64

Begin working chart at top right

Begin working chart at top right

Row 1

Chart B

□ White
■ Black
▫ Flesh
▨ Gold
▣ Red

Background: Royal

Row 32

VELVET AND NEEDLEPOINT STOCKING

*M*ake this richly worked needlepoint stocking for an extra-special person, and fill with personalised choice gifts to be cherished in years to come.

MATERIALS

20cm x 30cm (8in x 12in) Zweigart Stramin No 38 double canvas, 10 holes to 2.5cm (1in)
Tapestry needle size 18
Stranded tapisserie wool in shades detailed on colour key
Matching wool braid approximately 1.5m (60in) and tassel
20cm x 30cm (8in x 12in) piece of folded velvet
20cm x 30cm (8in x 12in) piece of folded lining
Our stocking measures approximately 28cm (11in) high and at the widest part of the foot 20.5cm (8in)

Mark the centre of the canvas lengthwise and breadthwise by folding in half and then in quarters, and sewing along the folds with running stitches. Stretch the canvas onto a tapestry frame and stitch in position to ensure the work does not become distorted.

Follow the charted design, working the background to fit your chosen stocking size; each square represents one stitch. Begin in the middle of the canvas, gradually working outwards in tent stitch.

To commence stitching, make a knot in end of wool, pull needle through canvas with the knot on right side about 2.5cm (1in) from the stitching point. Work stitches over to this point, securing wool 'tail' on reverse, then cut knot on front. *To finish off thread*, take needle through to back of canvas and weave through some previously sewn stitches.

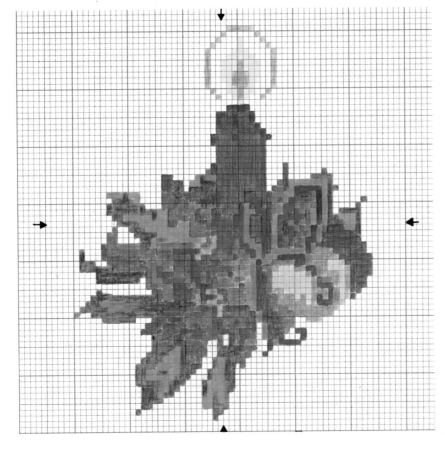

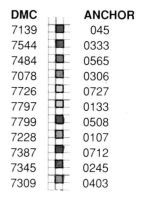

DMC		ANCHOR
7139		045
7544		0333
7484		0565
7078		0306
7726		0727
7797		0133
7799		0508
7228		0107
7387		0712
7345		0245
7309		0403

The chart is 54 stitches wide by 69 stitches deep

VELVET AND NEEDLEPOINT STOCKING

Remove the completed tapestry from the frame. The finished canvas will need blocking: spray the reverse lightly with water and pull to shape diagonally from each corner.

Cut out a stocking shape from it using the template from page 45 graded-up to the required size, and allowing 12mm (½in) seam allowance. Cut two pieces of lining fabric and one piece of velvet to same stocking size. Machine one piece of lining to worked tapestry piece at the top edge on the wrong side, repeat for velvet and other lining

piece. Press open the seams, lay the two stitched pieces on top of each other and machine around the outer edge, leaving a 10cm (4in) gap at the bottom edge to pull through to the right side. Clip up to the seamline around the curves and trim the excess fabric away.

Turn to the right side, press seams gently and close up opening with small stitches. Push the lining back down into the stocking, sew the braid on by hand, following the seam edge, and stitch the tassel to the left top edge.

GIANT MACHINE-KNIT STOCKING

Make this fun-sized stocking and hang at the end of a child's bed full of exciting gifts – then you can be sure of a lie-in in the morning!

MATERIALS

100g (4oz) red double knitting yarn
50g (2oz) cream double knitting yarn
Decoration: green and brown yarn, beads, star sequins, tartan ribbon
Tension: 27 stitches and 32 rows to 10cm (4in)
Machine: Any double-bed chunky machine, or use every other needle on a standard machine.

Cast on 110 sts (55 on each bed, observing the needle rule for your machine, and following your machine's instructions for circular knitting). Knit for 18cm (7in) in cream yarn, change to red yarn and knit 65cm (25in) then change to cream again and knit 30cm (12in) before casting off. To cast off, continue circular knitting in waste yarn for ten rounds and remove from the machine.

Fold the waste knitting to the outside and pick up the stitches by hand using a tapestry needle. Thread the needle into the last stitch and pull yarn to the right side, pick up the same stitch and the one on the back row, pulling yarn through. Continue around the circle in the same manner catching in all stitches, unravel waste yarn and sew in ends. Press knitting lightly.

Cut into the centre of the knitted tube at the lower edge up to the point where red and white colours meet on front and back of tube; turn the tube inside out and make mitred toe cap by joining up front and back sections with a machined dart. Cut away excess fabric.

Machine the top edge to neaten, turn down and stitch on the inside at colour change. Fold over to the front to make doubled turn-down. Knit a small loop by same method as stocking and stitch to the top for hanging.

Decorate with green wool, working large cross stitches to make the tree, blanket stitch for the pot, and sew on beads, sequins and ribbon for the trims.

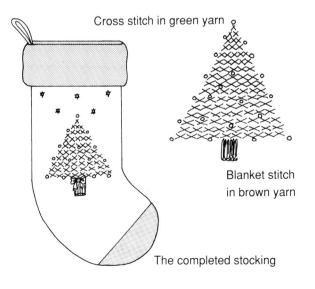

Cross stitch in green yarn

Blanket stitch in brown yarn

The completed stocking

SPICED CHRISTMAS TREE

*T*his would make an ideal gift, as there are two presents in one: not only is the tree everlasting, but the herbs and spices can be removed and used for cooking without spoiling the tree.

MATERIALS
The tree

40cm (16in) dry-foam cone
Wooden branch or stick 30cm (12in) long x 5cm (2in) diameter
Terracotta flowerpot 15.5cm (6in) deep x 20cm (8in) diameter
Large box of 'all purpose' plaster filler
Kitchen paper towel
Glue
Jamjar lid
2 cups of small gravel chippings

The decorations

4 white bunches sea lavender (*Statice dumosa*)
2 green bunches sea lavender
1 packet 17.5cm (7in) florist's stub wires
15 bundles of cinnamon sticks 8cm (3in) long
15 *bouquet garni* bundles in muslin
Plus: 15 red baubles 2.5cm (1in) in diameter, gold cherub, mini gold bells, mini cones, artificial red berries, 2m x 6mm (80in x 1/4in) gold ribbon, 1m x 10cm (40in x 4in) red ribbon, packet red crêpe paper

PREPARING THE BASE

Put the upturned jamjar lid in the base of the pot to prevent the filler from seeping out at the bottom. Line the pot with kitchen paper towel: this will prevent the pot from splitting when the filler dries out.

Following the manufacturer's instructions, mix the filler and fill up two-thirds of the pot with it. Embed the wooden branch or stick vertically into the mixture, pushing it down firmly to the bottom. Wedge in position and allow to set for a few hours.

Mix more filler and top up the pot to within 12mm (1/2in) of the brim. Before this sets cover the surface with gravel, gently pressing it into the filler. Allow to set for a further few hours before attaching the cone.

To fix the cone make a hole in the middle of its base, the same diameter as the branch or stick and 2.5cm (1in) deep. Cover the top of the branch/stick with glue and press the cone down well onto it to adhere properly.

DECORATING THE TREE

Insert 8cm (3in) lengths of white sea lavender horizontally into the cone, working around the base and then upwards towards the top. Gradually decrease the length of the stems as you reach the top; they should be no more than 5cm (2in) long and inserted at an angle towards the tip of the tree.

Set stick into pot

Insert first layer of sea lavender

The finished tree, complete with crêpe paper wrapper and ribbon bow

When the cone is well covered, insert the green lavender at random, ensuring that the overall appearance is balanced. The denser the arrangement the better.

Wire the cinnamon bundles together with the berries and cones (you can buy cinnamon already packed in small bundles with twine around them), and fix to the tree by winding the stub wires to them and then pushing these wires into

SPICED CHRISTMAS TREE

the cone. Attach a stub wire to the back of the cherub and position on the top of the tree.

Finally, wrap crêpe paper around the flowerpot and finish off with a big ribbon bow.

The tree can be stored for the following year by covering it with a plastic bag to keep off the dust. To rejuvenate, add some drops of cinnamon essence to the tree. A hairdrier on low setting will remove any dust that may accumulate if you keep the tree on display!

SEASONAL POMANDERS

Centuries ago pomanders were carried by the gentry to expel any nasty odours that might waft by as they walked the streets. Our versions will add pleasant scents to your rooms at Christmas.

MATERIALS

Clove Orange

Medium orange, cloves
Felt pen
1m (40in) red or green ribbon 12mm (^{1}/$_2$in) wide
1 teaspoon orris root
1 tablespoon allspice
Kitchen paper

Lace-trimmed Rosebud

Approximately 3 dozen tightly closed dried red rosebuds
Florist's scissors, florist's wire
Dry-foam ball 7.5cm (3in) in diameter
40cm (16in) scalloped lace 3cm (1^1/$_4$in) wide
Pearl beads
Glue
1m (40in) green velvet ribbon 3cm (1^1/$_4$in) wide
Rose essence

CLOVE ORANGE

Thin-skinned oranges give the best results. Mark the width of the ribbon on the orange from top to bottom with the felt pen. Insert cloves into the orange each side of the marked ribbon position, pushing in as many as you can. If you have diffi-

culties, use a skewer to make an initial hole.

Roll the orange in the orris root and spice mix, shake off excess and wrap in kitchen paper and keep in a cool dark place for four weeks. This will allow the perfumes to infuse and the orange to dry out. When ready, tie the ribbon around the orange and make a loop in it to hang up.

LACE-TRIMMED ROSEBUD

Cut the rosebuds off the stems leaving a stalk of 12mm (^{1}/$_2$in), and insert each bud all around the foam ball. For extra firmness, dab some glue on the cut end of the stalk before inserting.

Gather the lace up with small running stitches and sew ends of lace together to form a circle; sew a bead in the middle of each scallop. Fix to the top of the ball with wire. Make a hanging loop and bow from the velvet ribbon; glue bow to base of loop and wire loop to top of ball above lace. Add drops of essence to the lace for fragrance.

A Victorian posy
Make a Victorian posy by using a florist's doily and wiring into it a bunch of dried flowers, cinnamon sticks and star aniseed.

KISSING BOUGH

*I*n Victorian times a version of this would grace many a hallway and guests would be greeted under it with a 'welcome kiss'. By using artificial mistletoe yours can be used year after year without losing its freshness.

MATERIALS

3 wire hoops 48cm (19in) in diameter
3 x 3m (120in) lengths of gold tinsel
3 stems of mistletoe each 25cm (10in) long
4 candles 15cm (6in) long, 4 clip-on candle-holders
Fine florist's wire
1m (40in) red ribbon 8cm (3in) wide
Sticky tape

Wrap each length of tinsel in a tight spiral around one of the hoops. Fix the ends with sticky tape. Wire two hoops together to form a sphere, then wire the third hoop horizontally in the middle of the other hoops. Attach the stems of mistletoe with wire under the central join at the top, hanging down inside the hoops.

Make a full bow at the bottom. Clip a candle-holder to the horizontal bar in each of the four sections, and position the candles in them. Make a hanging loop of wire and fix to the top of the bough. Hang in a suitable place.

> **SAFETY FIRST** Never *allow the candles to burn down near the tinsel.*

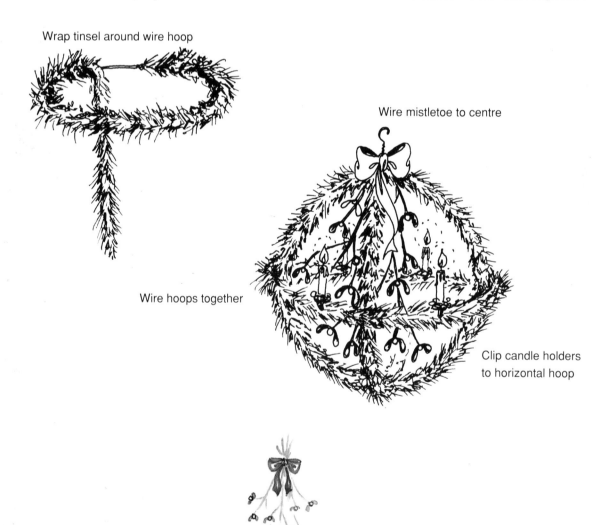

Wrap tinsel around wire hoop

Wire mistletoe to centre

Wire hoops together

Clip candle holders to horizontal hoop

POINSETTIA PLANT IN FIR CONE-DECORATED BASKET

This basket looks good with a real plant or one made from silk. You could also use an arrangement of luscious fruit.

MATERIALS

Basket with long handle – ours is 12cm (5in)
deep x 40cm (16in) diameter
80 small fir cones approximately 6cm (2¹/₂in)
long (available from large garden centres)
Fine florist's wire, wire cutter
Varnish, paintbrush
Fresh or artificial poinsettia plant
1m (40in) red ribbon 10cm (4in) wide

Cut 25cm (10in) lengths of wire and wrap in and out of the base of each cone, with a length free to wire them to the basket. Beginning at the bottom of the basket, wire a cone onto the left side of handle. Twist the wire through to the back and wrap around several times to secure the cone. Follow this method all the way around the base of the basket, beginning the next row above the first cone and working a further two rows as before.

Varnish the cones with two coats of clear varnish. Sit potted plant in this decorated basket, and trim the handle with ribbon or a bought rosette.

FABRIC WELCOME GARLAND

This cheery garland is an ideal decoration for inner doors. Make it in colourful co-ordinating prints, or for a glamorous effect try it in gold lurex fabric with a red bow.

MATERIALS

3 strips of fabric 1.5m (60in) long and 13cm
(5in) wide
Polyester wadding
1m (40in) red satin ribbon 8cm (3in) wide
1m (40in) red spotted ribbon 4cm (1¹/₂in) wide
Spray-on glue
Bell trim
Brass curtain ring

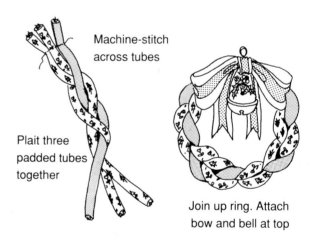

Machine-stitch across tubes

Plait three padded tubes together

Join up ring. Attach bow and bell at top

Fold each strip in half lengthways and machine-stitch down the long edges, on the wrong side of the fabric, taking 12mm (¹/₂in) seam allowance. Trim the seams and turn tubes to the right side; pack each tube firmly with wadding to within 4cm (1¹/₂in) of each end. Machine the three tubes together at one end. Plait the three joined pieces together. Stitch ends of plait together to join up the ring.

Spray glue on the reverse side of the spotted ribbon and glue to the right side of the red ribbon, in the middle down its length. Make a big bow and sew over the joins on the garland. Sew the bell in position under the bow. Sew the curtain-ring on the reverse of the plait at the top to hang the garland.

SANTA CLAUS IN SALT DOUGH

Your family beware: this charming craft could cost them their Christmas lunch. Once you begin it you will become so hooked that your oven will be brimming over with ideas!

MATERIALS

1 cup salt, 1 cup water
3 cups plain flour
Baking parchment
Garlic press, rolling pin
Hardboard for frame backing; wooden frame
Felt pen
Clear varnish
Wooden cocktail sticks and barbecue sticks
Pompon
Watercolour paints and brush
Ready-mixed wall-tile adhesive

Mix the salt, flour and water in a bowl, form into a dough by kneading with your knuckles. Leave for a few minutes to settle. Before making your design, assemble all the items to assist with the construction before your hands are covered with flour.

SANTA CLAUS

Roll out a ball of dough 5cm (2in) in diameter. Flatten between palms, keeping a circular outline. Make a rectangle for the body approximately 5cm (2in) wide x 6cm (2½in) long. Insert half a cocktail stick by pushing it into the top of the body edge. Join this to the head by wetting the edge of the circle and gently pushing the remaining half into it on the edge.

With head and body joined, flour a work surface to begin building up the rest of the design. Mould two triangles of dough approximately 6cm (2½in) long for the arms, bend into position and fix to the body with water. Make two small balls for the hands, and indent with a cocktail stick for the thumb. The green sack is made from a piece of dough squashed flat into an oval, and a gathered bit at the top for the hand to clasp. Attach the sack under the left arm by wetting both surfaces and resting the arm on top of it. Make a strip for the belt, a tiny ball for the button and a square for the belt buckle and fix these on with water.

For the legs make two rectangles 2.5cm (1in) x 3cm (1¼in), cut the barbecue sticks in half and push right through the length of the pieces of dough. Join to the base of the body as before.

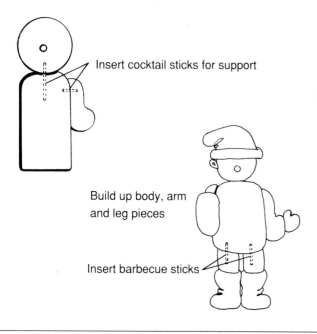

Insert cocktail sticks for support

Build up body, arm and leg pieces

Insert barbecue sticks

Add dough pushed through garlic press for beard

Santa Claus complete with sack of toys. Cook before painting

SANTA CLAUS IN SALT DOUGH

Mould two pieces of dough for the boots 6cm (2^{1}/$_{2}$in) long, 3cm (1^{1}/$_{4}$in) across and widening to 3.5cm (1^{1}/$_{2}$in) at the base. Attach to the bottom of the legs.

For the moustache and beard squeeze the dough through a garlic press and arrange as in the photograph. Make a small ball for the nose and a tinier one for the mouth; fix onto the face with water. Make two ears, indent with the blunt end of a barbecue stick in both the ears and to mark the mouth. Roll out a triangle of dough for the hat and a strip for the brim; attach as before.

SANTA'S SACK OF TOYS

Flatten a piece of dough to resemble the yellow sack. Roll a ball for teddy's head, and small balls for his nose, ears and mouth. Make two paws and a body and fix the head pieces in position under the top edge of the sack. Make a sausage of dough, bend over at one end for the stick of rock and add to the sack. With a fish slice, lift the completed design onto a tin lined with baking parchment and bake in a cool oven for three hours.

When completely dry paint with watercolour paints, beginning with the skin tones and following with the other colours. Draw in the eyes and the bear's paws with a felt pen. Paint all over with two coats of varnish. Cut hardboard to 25cm (10in) x 18cm (7in) and glue the design onto it using the wall-tile adhesive. Glue pompon to hat at the end, then glue the flat surface of the figure to the hardboard. When thoroughly dry, mount the hardboard in the frame.

▼ *Santa Claus in Salt Dough, with examples of Choir Boy and Girl variations*

FATHER CHRISTMAS MOBILE

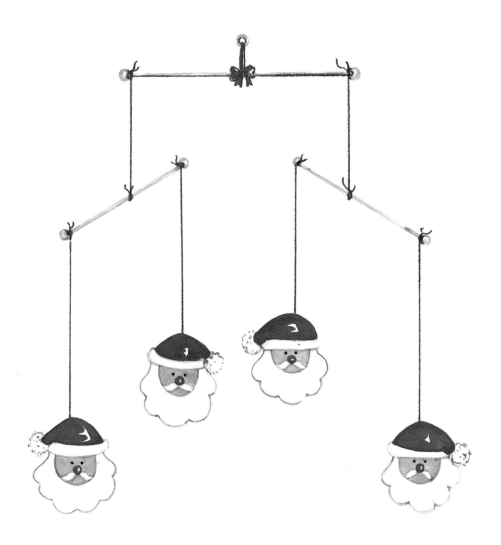

This jolly mobile can be made in minutes, and can easily be adapted to make a lovely gift for a newborn baby, as on page 129.

MATERIALS

Assorted pieces of felt in red, white and skin colours

Tracing paper, card

Ribbon 20cm x 6mm (8in x 1/4in)

4 pompons

1 plastic curtain ring

3 sticks (bamboo skewers) approximately 25cm (10in) long

Cotton thread

6 wooden beads

Glue

Trace the shapes onto card and cut two of each shape in appropriate coloured felt for one complete Santa's head. See pattern pieces for colour reference.

Beginning with one face piece, glue a white beard piece onto the bottom of it, overlapping slightly. Then glue a red hat piece onto the top edge of the face. Where the hat meets the face glue a white hat brim, and glue a red nose in the middle of the face. Repeat the same method for the back of the Santa, reversing the pieces as you stick them.

Now stick the two heads together, enclosing a 30cm (12in) length of thread at the top for hanging to the mobile frame. Sew a pompon to the end of each four hat pieces. Draw on eyes with felt pen.

FATHER CHRISTMAS MOBILE

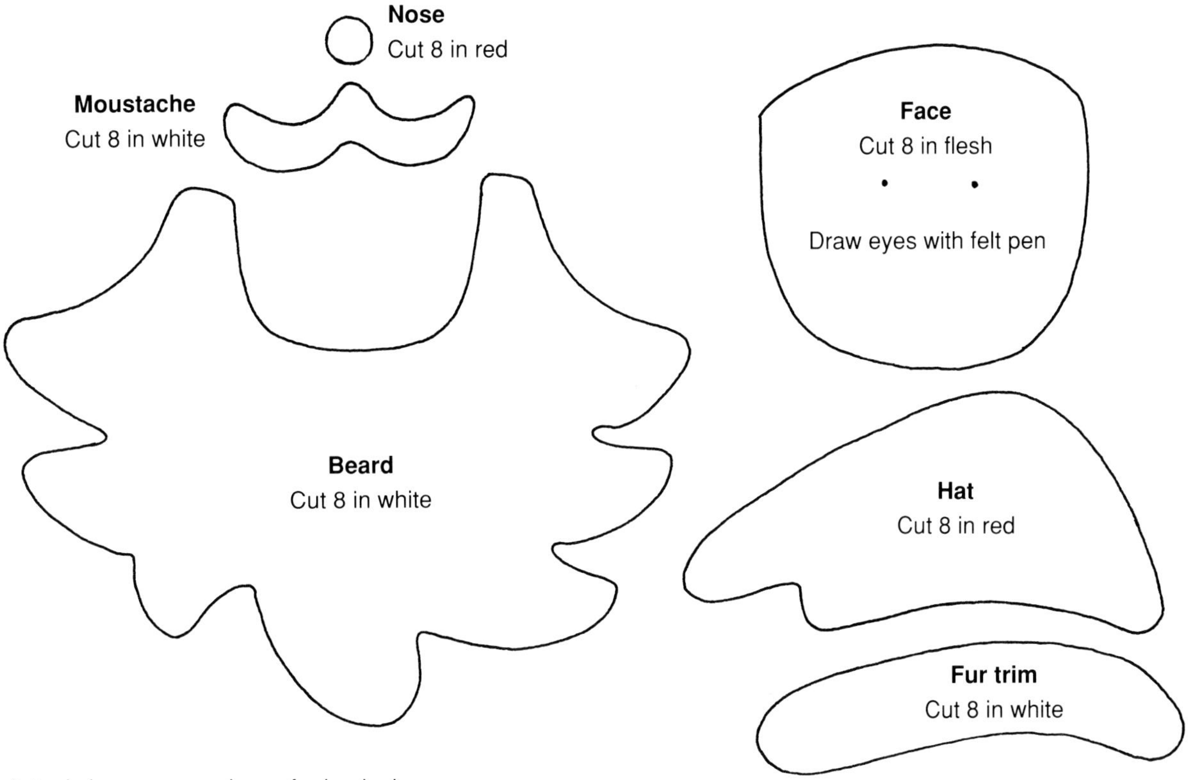

Nose
Cut 8 in red

Moustache
Cut 8 in white

Face
Cut 8 in flesh

Draw eyes with felt pen

Beard
Cut 8 in white

Hat
Cut 8 in red

Fur trim
Cut 8 in white

Actual size: reverse pieces for back view

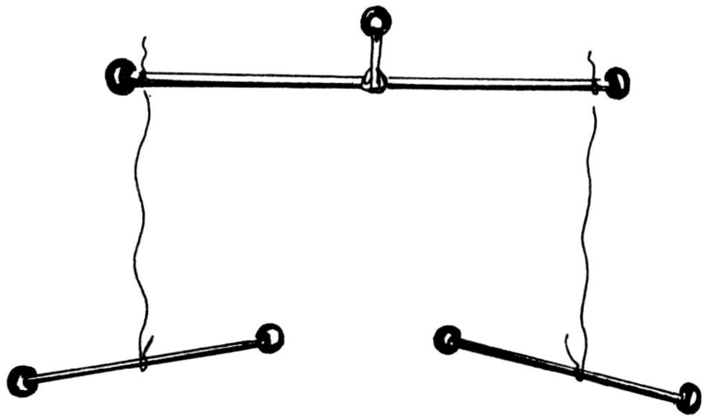

Tie strings in positions shown

MOBILE FRAME

Cut one stick to 24cm (9½in) and the other two each to 18cm (7in) long by cutting off the pointed ends. Glue a wooden bead to each end of the three sticks. Loop the ribbon over the middle of the long stick, sew a curtain-ring to it for hanging, and tie a 20cm (8in) length of thread to each end of it.

Then tie one short stick to the end of each thread.

Take each Santa head with its attached thread and tie one to each end of the shorter sticks, ensuring all threads are of equal length. To balance the mobile, simply adjust the position of the threads along the length of the stick.

Reminder: All mobiles should be hung out of reach of babies and small children.

ADVENT GIFT BASKET

*M*ake this simple basket to hide your advent gifts: at the end of the numbered tag is a welcome surprise. You could turn it into a present by filling with an assortment of toiletries or items for a keen gardener.

MATERIALS

Fruit pannier/basket
1.25m (50in) gathered broderie anglaise 5cm (2in) wide
30cm (12in) glazed cotton 90cm (36in) wide
3m (120in) narrow piping cord
24 card discs 4 cm (2in) diameter and a hole punch
1.25m (50in) each 2cm (^{3}/4in) wide and 5cm (2in) wide tartan ribbon
Green acrylic paint and brush
Glue
(Above quantities are for a basket measuring approximately 36cm (14in) long x 25cm (10in) wide x 12cm (5in) deep. Measure your basket to gauge your required quantities.)

Paint the outside of the basket and the handle in green. Cut a strip of fabric long enough and wide enough to fit the edge of the basket – allow 4 cm (1^1/2in) at the top edge to hem and make a channel for a drawstring.

Seam ends of the strip together on the wrong side, machine top edge for drawstring and insert some cord piping for drawing up. Glue the right side along the raw edges of the strip to the inside top edge of the basket. Glue the broderie anglaise to the outside of the basket along the top edge, and glue tartan ribbon over the straight edge of the broderie. Spiral tartan ribbon around the handle and glue in place. Make tartan bows and glue onto the sides at base of handles.

Punch a hole in each card disc, cut the cord to assorted lengths, and thread each length through a card disc, knotting on the other side. Tie each card to a gift that is hidden in the basket. Write numbers 1–24 on the discs to complete.

Channel for drawstring

Glue fabric to inner edge of basket

Glue on broderie anglaise

Attach ties and number discs

WALL-HANGING ADVENT CALENDAR

Make this charming scene, reminiscent of a Victorian Christmas card, and delight the family. Children will certainly find it tempting as they receive a small gift each day in the run-up to Christmas. It is guaranteed to bring as much pleasure the first moment they set eyes on it as in subsequent years.

MATERIALS

2m (80in) natural hessian fabric 115cm (45in) wide

4m (160in) red bias binding 5cm (2in) wide

1.5cm (60in) red bias binding 2.5cm (1in) wide

20 brass curtain-rings

1m (40in) red satin ribbon 7.5cm (3in) wide

Snowflake sequins and star sequins

96cm (38in) length of wood, 4cm (1^1/$_2$in) wide

2 wooden knobs, with flat base 4cm (1^1/$_2$in) diameter

1.5m (60in) red cord 6mm (^{1}/$_4$in) thick

3m (120in) red ribbon 6mm (^{1}/$_4$in) wide

2 brass bells, 6.5cm (2^1/$_2$in) diameter

Card and tracing paper

Glue

Saw

Assorted scraps of felt in red, black, dark green, brown, camel, chestnut, dark grey, lilac, cerise, mustard

35cm (14in) white felt 90cm (36in) wide

40cm (16in) pale grey felt 90cm (36in) wide

Fabric pen in black

10cm (4in) cerise ribbon 3mm (^{1}/$_8$in) wide

Cut two oblongs of the hessian 1m (40in) long x 84cm (33in) wide. With one piece on top of the other, neaten the edges by folding the 5cm (2in)-width bias binding over them and machine close to inner edge on the two long sides and one short side. Cut four straps of hessian 22cm (9in) long and 6cm (2^1/$_2$in) wide; bind each long edge with 2.5cm (1in)-width binding. Fold straps in half, space evenly across the top and machine in position. Turn the hessian over and machine a folded piece of 5cm (2in) binding across the front top edge. Press the hanging; it is now ready to decorate.

Saw wood to fit across the top with a small overlap for knobs and ties. Glue wooden knobs to each end, and tie red cord to one knob. Insert wood through the loops at the top of the hanging. Knot the other end of the cord to the opposite knob.

Trace and grade up the shapes (see Techniques) and make card templates of them, then use these to cut out in felt. Machine strip of icicles across the top, the frozen lake in the middle and the pockets at the bottom. Stitch brass rings at random on the front of the hanging. Cut out felt numbers or use a marker pen and number the rings and pockets.

Glue on the felt shapes as in the photograph on pages 8–9, remembering to work from the bottom layer upwards when sticking several layers on top of each other. For example, stick the dark green felt for the tree before adding the white for the snow and the stars. Draw features and skates with fabric marker pen. Tie bow on lady's hat and stitch bows to the top left and right side of hanging. Loop some ribbon through the bells and stitch to hanging, under the bows. To attach your gifts, wrap them into small parcels and tie to the rings with the narrow ribbon.

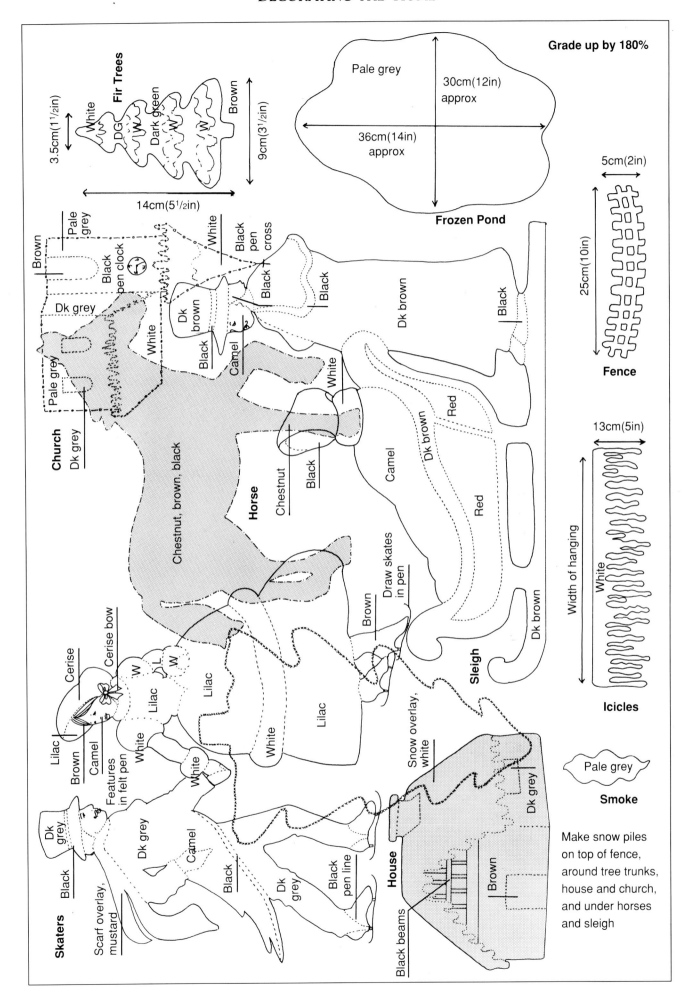

Fir Trees

White
DG
Dark green
W
W
W
Brown

3.5cm(1½in)
9cm(3½in)
14cm(5½in)

Grade up by 180%

Pale grey
30cm(12in) approx
36cm(14in) approx

Frozen Pond

5cm(2in)
25cm(10in)

Fence

Brown
Pale grey
Black pen clock
Dk grey
Pale grey
Church
Dk grey

White
Black pen cross
Dk brown
Black
Black
Camel
Black

Dk brown

Black

White
Chestnut, brown, black
Horse
Chestnut
Black
White

Dk brown
Red
Camel
Red

13cm(5in)
Width of hanging
White
Icicles

Cerise bow
Cerise
W
L
W
Lilac
Lilac
White
Lilac
Brown
Draw skates in pen

Lilac
Brown
Camel
Features in felt pen
White
White
White
Snow overlay, white

Dk brown
Sleigh

Pale grey
Smoke

Dk grey
Black
Camel
Black
Dk grey
Black pen line
House
Black beams
Brown
Dk grey

Skaters
Scarf overlay, mustard

Make snow piles on top of fence, around tree trunks, house and church, and under horses and sleigh

31

CHAPTER TWO

THE CHRISTMAS TREE AND CRIB

CHRISTMAS TREE MAT

*T*his is a very useful item to make if you have a real Christmas tree, as it will catch the pine needles when they drop. It would look just as good under an artificial tree with all the presents.

MATERIALS

1m (40in) unbleached twill cotton fabric 140cm (54in) wide
4m (160in) of red bias binding 5cm (2in) wide
Stencil parchment, sharp craft knife
Stencil paints and brush
String and drawing pin
Tracing paper

Fold fabric in half and again into quarters. Knot the string around the stem of a drawing pin, lay fabric on carpet or work surface and stick pin into the top point of folded edge. Tie a pencil to other end of string, then, holding it taut, draw a curve from one edge of fabric to the other. Cut out along the curve. Open out fabric to form a circle. Fold binding in half over the raw edge of the circle and machine all the way around, turning the binding in at the end to neaten.

Press the mat with an iron before you stencil it, ensuring that it is crease-free for printing. Trace the motif from the book onto stencil parchment; carefully cut out the design with a sharp craft knife. Ensure that all the edges are smooth: a fine emery board can be used to remove any roughness. Position the stencil 5cm (2in) in from the bound edge. Working with one colour at a time, begin to fill the bell in with yellow stencil paint. Work the brush in a dabbing up-and-down or stippling movement; any narrow areas can be filled in with a stiff paintbrush. Be careful not to move the stencil as you paint or the finished work will blur. It may be helpful to tape the stencil onto the fabric or weigh it down as you work over it.

Lift the stencil off carefully and clean it with a cloth dipped in soapy water, reposition about 15cm (6in) from previous stencilled bell design

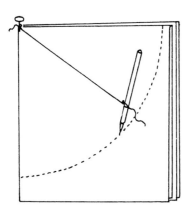

Pin string to secure. Hold taut to draw curve

Cut out stencil using a sharp craft knife

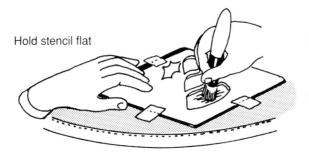

Hold stencil flat

Stipple paint

Tape stencil to cloth

CHRISTMAS TREE MAT

and work as before. Continue in this way until ten bell designs have been stencilled around the circle, remembering to clean the stencil after each print. Next, stencil the ribbon in red on all previously worked designs, followed by green for the holly leaves, keeping to the same procedure as before.

Heat set the design onto the fabric with a hot iron following the maker's instructions: this enables the mat to be washed.

Tip: If you cannot find parchment in your local art shop, you can make your own proofed card with a solution of linseed oil and turpentine. Measure equal amounts of both oil and turpentine into an old tin and boil for five minutes. When cool, paint the card with the mixture using a broad soft brush to distribute it evenly. Allow to dry before using.

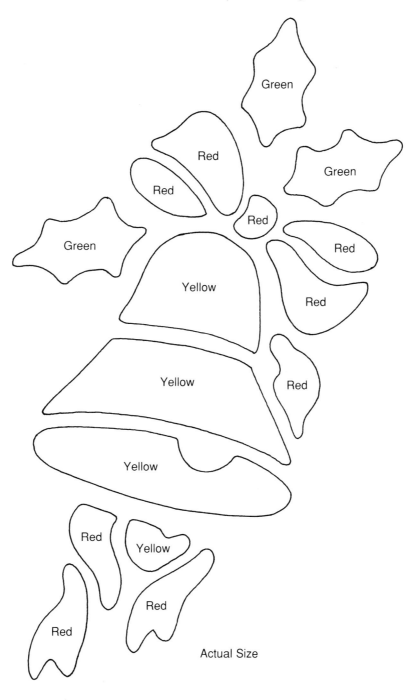

Actual Size

CROSS STITCH
SANTA STOCKING

MATERIALS

20cm (8in) square Zweigart Aida cloth no 3706
14 holes to 2.5cm (1in)
20cm (8in) square of felt
Stranded embroidery cotton in colours detailed
on colour key
70cm (27in) bias binding 12mm (^{1}/2in) wide
Tapestry needle size 24
Our stocking measures 15cm (6in) high and
14cm (5^1/2in) at the widest part of the foot.

Square up Aida fabric by folding into quarters and marking each quarter with tacking threads. Stretch fabric in a hoop or frame (a small wooden picture frame can be used, with drawing pins to secure). If using a hoop, line up the adjuster bolt with top central thread. Beginning in the centre, follow the motif from the chart in cross stitch (see Techniques). Work with three strands of cotton in your needle throughout.

When complete, press gently on the reverse, then cut out stocking shape in both canvas and felt, using the shape on page 45 graded to the size of stocking required. Machine folded strip of binding across the top of each stocking piece, enclosing raw edges. Lay canvas on top of felt, pin folded bias binding around outer edge enclosing raw edges of both pieces, and allowing an extension on one side of 6cm (2^1/2in) for a hanging loop. Machine close to unfolded edge. Turn back loop at top and hand-sew down. Press to finish.

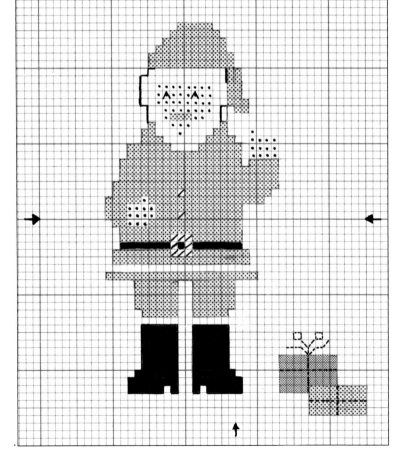

The chart is 36 stitches wide by
52 stitches deep

DMC		ANCHOR
729	▦	874
310	■	403
3779	⊡	778
666	▥	334
904	▨	245
—		Back stitch 310/403
---		Gold thread back stitch

DRIED FLOWER TREE ORNAMENTS

F or an unusual selection of tree ornaments make these with dried flowers and basket shapes. Spray gold or leave natural to vary the effect.

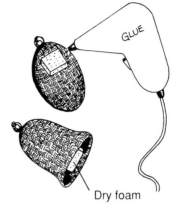

Glue dry foam to basket shape

Dry foam

MATERIALS

Selection of basket shapes: oval, fan, bell, pram
Assorted dried flowers and seedheads
Dry-foam pieces
Gold spray paint
Glue
1m (40in) ribbon 6mm (^{1}/4in) wide

GOLD ORNAMENTS

Spray both basket shapes and some of the dried flowers with the gold paint. Glue small pieces of dry foam onto the baskets as a base for inserting the dried flowers. Cut flowers, seed pods etc to assorted lengths and push into the foam to form a balanced arrangement. Fix a ribbon hanging loop at the top of each ornament.

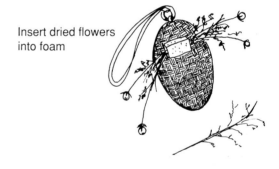

Insert dried flowers into foam

WOODEN TREE DECORATIONS

These decorations look as good in the colourways photographed on pages 32-3, or in an assortment of primary colours. They are simple to make, but if you are short of time you can buy pre-cut wooden shapes to paint yourself.

Trace shapes from the book onto the wood. Cut out, following the instructions as for the clown on page 114. Bought shapes were used to make the angel and the heart decoration. Paint ornaments with chosen colours, and when dry drill holes in the top to secure the ribbon for hanging to the tree.

MATERIALS

A piece of 6mm (^{1}/4in) multicore plywood
Fretsaw
Table clamps
Drill and 3.5mm (^{1}/8in) drill bit
Sandpaper, tracing paper
Glue
1m (40in) ribbon 6mm (^{1}/4in) wide
Acrylic paints and brush

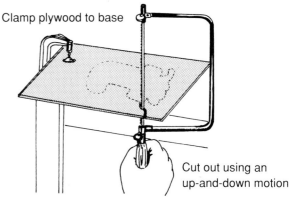

Clamp plywood to base

Cut out using an up-and-down motion

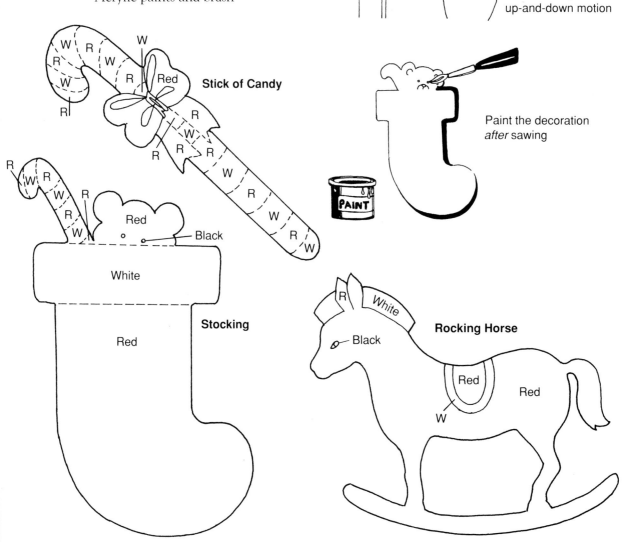

Stick of Candy

Paint the decoration *after* sawing

PAINT

Red
White
Black
Stocking
Red

Rocking Horse
White
Black
Red
Red
W

VICTORIAN CROCHET TREE ORNAMENTS

MATERIALS

200g (8oz) ball cotton crochet yarn Anchor
Pelicano No 5 white
Cold water dye to colour your finished products
for coloured ornaments
1.25mm crochet hook (UK 3, USA 8)
Trims for decorating: ribbon bows, ribbon roses,
dried flowers
Small amount of polyester wadding for bell
Sugar and water stiffening solution (see page 85)
(For crochet terms and methods, see Techniques)

BASKET

Row 1: 6 ch, close into a ring with a slip stitch.
Row 2: 3 ch, 20 trb into ring, 1 slp st in third ch of
first 3 ch to close.
Row 3: 1 ch, 20 dc around, 1 slp st in first ch to
close.
Row 4: 1 ch, 22 dc around, 1 slp st in first ch to
close.

Row 5: * 3 ch, miss 1 ch below, 1 dc into next ch,
repeat after * until 12 loops formed, 3 ch, 1 slp st
into first ch at beginning.
Row 6: 1 ch, * 1 dc, 1 htrb, 1 trb, 1 htrb, 1 dc into
loop below, slp st into next loop, 1 dc repeat after
* 11 times, slp st in first ch to close. 12 loops.
Row 7: 5 ch, * 1 dc in ch below, 3 ch, repeat after
* 11 times slp st into third ch at beginning to
close. 13 loops.
Row 8: 3 ch, slp st in ch below to form picot, * 3
dc, 1 slp st, 3 ch and 1 slp st into loop, repeat 13
times after * 3 dc. In last loop 1 slp st in first picot
to close, 14 picots.
Fasten off yarn.

HANDLE

Pick up a stitch from second row down at the side
on the inside of basket and make 31 ch stitches.
Slip st back along ch 30 times and pick up
another st from side of basket. 1 ch turn dc back

VICTORIAN CROCHET TREE ORNAMENTS

along 30 slp st below, fasten off yarn. Sew the end of the handle to the inside of other side of basket. Catch attached side of handle to the inside with small stitches, sew in loose threads. Stiffen the handle with some sugar and water solution and allow to harden. Glue on ribbon trim and fill with assorted colour co-ordinated dried flowers.

FAN

Row 1: 6 ch, slp st to close into a ring.
Row 2: 3 ch, 9 trb into ring, 3 ch turn.
Row 3: 1 dc in first trb below, * 2 ch miss 1 ch below 1 dc repeat 4 times after *, 3 ch turn.
Row 4: * 5 ch, 1 dc in next hole repeat after * 4 times, 5 ch turn.
Row 5: 3 trb through fifth chain from hook, (3 ch, 3 trb, 3 ch, 3 trb, 3 ch, 3 trb all in first hole below) repeat sequence in brackets four times, slp st in chain below to close up.
Row 6: 1 ch, 9 dc along bottom edge, 2 dc in ring, make 16 ch and slp st back along the chain. Slp st into the ring to form a loop, 2 dc in ring, 9 dc along other edge. Slp st at end, fasten off.

Sew in loose threads. Stiffen the main section of the fan (not the loop) with sugar solution, pinch the crochet at the wide end to make a frill. When hard, glue on a ribbon rose below the chain loop.

GARLAND

Row 1: 15 ch, slp st to close into a ring, 3 ch.
Row 2: Trb 37 times into the ring, 1 slp st to close.
Row 3: 3 ch, 16 trb around ring, 1 trb in last ch to increase, trb 4, 1 trb in last ch to increase, dc 7, 1 trb in last ch to increase, trb 4, 1 trb in last ch to increase, trb 5 (total 40 sts). Slp st into third chain to close.
Row 4: 3ch, * miss 1 ch below, 1 dc into next chain, 3 ch repeat after * to make 21 loops, 3 ch and slp st to end. Make 26 ch from hook, slp st into the first ch to make a hanging loop. Fasten off thread.

Sew in loose ends. Cover the garland with sugar solution, leave the loop and allow to harden. Glue on five ribbon roses, evenly spaced around the middle of the ring.

BELL

Row 1: 6 ch slp st to close into a ring.
Row 2: 8 dc into ring, 1 slp st into first dc to close up.
Row 3: 1 ch, 1 dc 10 times, join with a slp st to first dc.
Row 4: 1 ch, 11 dc join up with a slp st to first dc.
Row 5: 1 ch, 12 dc join up to first dc with a slp st.
Row 6: 1 ch, 14 dc, join up with a slp st to first dc.
Row 7: 13 dc, join up to first dc with a slp st.
Row 8: 11 dc, join up with a slp st to first dc.
Row 9: 10 dc, join up with a slp st to first dc.
Row 10: 8 dc, join up with a slp st to first dc.
Row 11: dc 8 times around base of handle, join up with a slp st.
Row 12: 5 ch, miss 1 ch below, 1 dc, 5 ch, 1 dc, miss 1 ch below 1 dc. 5 ch close up by slp st into second of first 5 ch.
Row 13: 1 ch, 20 dc around circle join up to first dc with a slp st.
Row 14: 3 ch, 20 dc around circle, slp st to first dc to close.
Row 15: 1 ch, 21 dc, join up with a slp st.
Row 16: 1 ch, 22 dc, join up with a slp st.
Row 17: 1 ch, 24 dc, join with a slp st to close.
Row 18: 5 ch, * miss 1 dc, 5 ch, repeat after * 11 times, 5 ch, slp st in second ch to 115 sts then close up.
Row 19: 5 ch, 1 dc into following loop to form new loops, repeat making 14 loops, 5 ch, join with a slp st to second ch of first 5 to close up.
Row 20: 1 ch, 50 dc spaced evenly around the ring, slp st to first dc to close up, fasten off yarn.

Make 15 ch with some yarn, ch 3, close up 3 ch with a slp st. 5 trb into ring and fasten off; this forms the bell-clapper. Sew this to the inside of the bell.

Make a chain hanging loop as for the garland. Fasten off yarn and sew in loose ends. Wad the handle of the bell with polyester wadding. Sit the bell on a mould, eg an upturned egg cup. Paint sugar solution around the handle and the top dc section of the bell, and allow to set hard before easing off the mould. Glue on a ribbon bow trim.

▶ *Victorian Crochet and Satin Tree Ornaments*

VICTORIAN TREE ORNAMENTS IN SATIN

*T*hese pretty ornaments can be made to colour co-ordinate with your other decorations; or you can bring them up to date by using pretty Provençal prints.

MATERIALS

(For three ornaments)
Satin fabric 25cm (10in) x 90cm (36in)
Scrap of felt
1m (40in) braid 12mm (^{1}/$_2$in) wide
2 small pearl beads for eyes, 1 drop pearl bead
70cm (27in) scalloped lace 2.5cm (1in) wide
23cm (9in) wood dowelling, 6mm (^{1}/$_4$in) diameter
1m (40in) ribbon 3mm (^{1}/$_8$in) wide
Polyester wadding
Glue
Tracing paper

Trace patterns from the book onto paper, then use to cut out two of each piece in satin, and two ears and one beak in felt.

BIRD

Pin body sections, right sides together; machine-stitch 6mm (^{1}/$_4$in) from edge and leave open at marked points. Repeat with wing sections. On curved edges, trim up to seam at 2.5cm (1in) intervals. Turn to the right side, pushing out points with a blunt instrument. Wad the body section well and the wing lightly, close up openings with small back stitches. Sew braid around the outer edge of the body and wing, covering the seam. Stitch lace to lower edge of the wing, then stitch wing to body in marked position. Sew on bead for eye and a ribbon hanging loop.

HOBBY HORSE

Make in same manner as for the bird, but leave seam open at the bottom to insert wood dowelling. Glue ribbon in a spiral around the dowelling, dab some glue to one end and insert this into open end of padded head section. Close opening with small stitches. Sew on felt ears, eye and ribbon halter. Gather lace and sew on for mane and sew on hanging loop.

BELL

Gather lace and machine in position on front of bell where marked. Lay other bell piece, right side down, on top of this and follow making instructions for the bird. Sew pearl drop bead at the base of the bell, and a ribbon hanging loop at the top.

In Victorian England popular tree ornaments were small items of embroidery, miniatures such as dolls, books, soldiers and – most popular – sugared fruits and nuts; these were kept for Twelfth Night, when all the decorations were taken down.

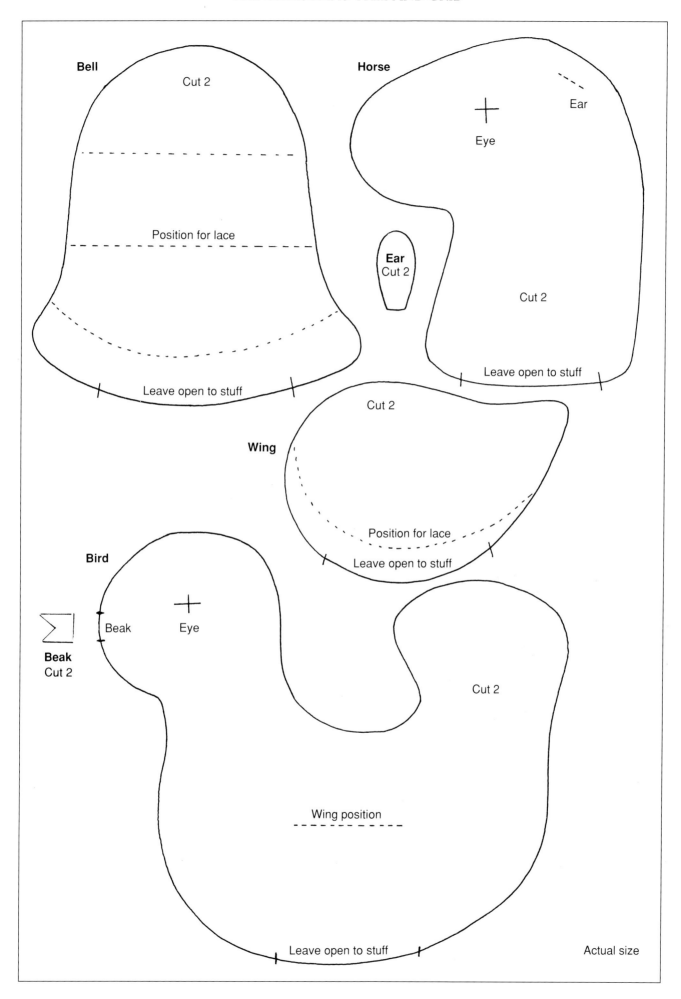

Bell

Cut 2

Position for lace

Leave open to stuff

Horse

Eye

Ear

Ear
Cut 2

Cut 2

Leave open to stuff

Cut 2

Wing

Position for lace

Leave open to stuff

Bird

Beak

Eye

Beak
Cut 2

Cut 2

Wing position

Leave open to stuff

Actual size

43

FELT AND FABRIC TREE ORNAMENTS

*T*hese winsome decorations would also make special gifts if filled with pot pourri. The stocking could carry a small gift or some sweets.

MATERIALS

Scraps of Christmas-printed fabric, colour co-ordinating plain fabric and felt pieces
Brass curtain rings 5cm (2in) diameter
2.5cm (1in) wide broderie anglaise
6mm (1/4in) wide ribbon
Wadding
Glue
Pinking shears
Tracing paper, card
Rosebud trims
Pot pourri/lavender

Trace shapes from the book onto paper and cut out one in fabric and one in felt for each design.

TREE

Place right side of print down onto the felt and machine 6mm (1/4in) in from the edge, leaving open at the bottom for wadding. Snip up to seam line on curves. Turn to the right side, fill with wadding and lavender, and close up the seam with small stitches. Gather a small rosette of broderie anglaise and sew in position with the rosebud on top. Sew on hanging loop.

HEART

Work as for the tree, but machine on the right side of fabric, instead of sewing on wrong side and turning through. Pink all around the outer edge through both layers. Finish off and sew on trims and loop as for the above.

STOCKING

Lay a strip of broderie anglaise across wrong side of top edge of the print piece of fabric. Machine across the top close to the raw edges. Fold over to the right side and press the seam flat. Lay the felt piece on top of right side of print piece. Cut a 20cm (8in) length of ribbon, fold in half and insert loop into the seam from the right side of fabric. Machine all the way around, turn stocking to the right side and press machined edge flat.

PICTURES

Cut one felt circle, one card circle and one print motif to fit the diameter of the brass ring. Glue print circle to the card circle, seam ends of broderie and gather up to a ring, then glue on the reverse of card circle. Glue the print side of trimmed card circle to the brass ring and on the reverse of this circle glue the felt circle to neaten. Tie ribbon for hanging, and glue on rosebud trim.

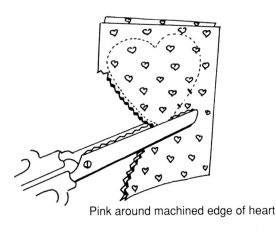

Pink around machined edge of heart

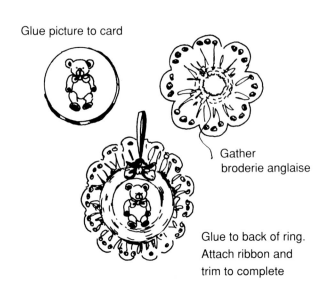

Glue picture to card

Gather broderie anglaise

Glue to back of ring. Attach ribbon and trim to complete

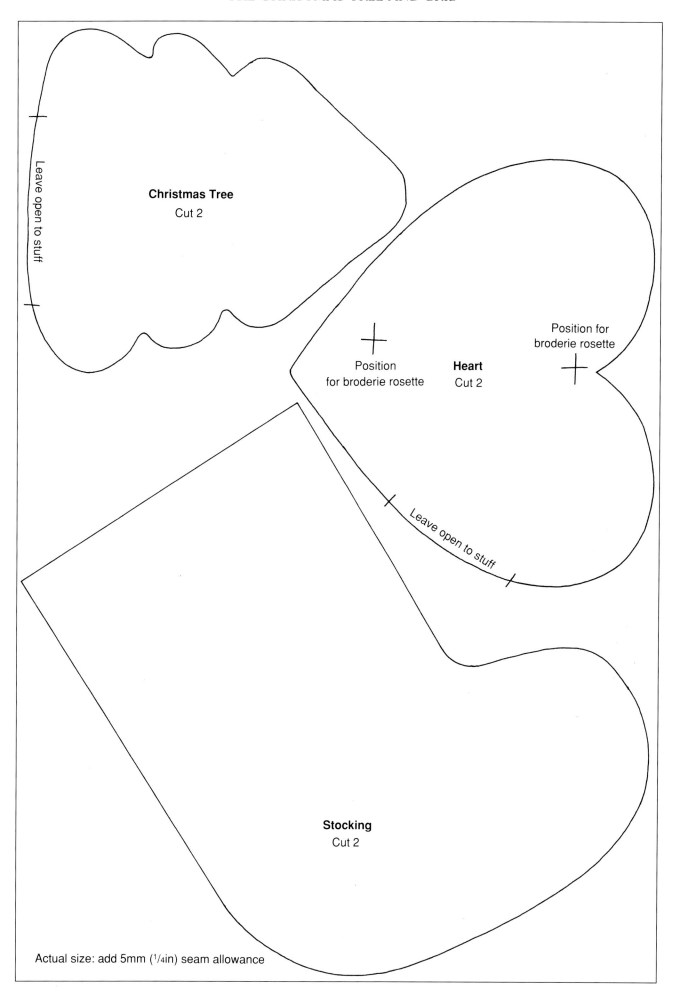

Christmas Tree
Cut 2

Leave open to stuff

Position
for broderie rosette

Heart
Cut 2

Position for
broderie rosette

Leave open to stuff

Stocking
Cut 2

Actual size: add 5mm (1/4in) seam allowance

NATIVITY SCENE

With a few household items this realistic scene can be made in next to no time. The cloth sculpture can be developed by using textures and colours to achieve a variety of effects.

MATERIALS

50cm (20in) piece of fabric such as lightweight plain cotton or cotton twill in beige
1 sheet of wrapping tissue paper
Cotton wool
8 cream pipe cleaners
Sheet of A2 59cm x 41cm (23³/8in x 16¹/2in) white card
3 x 5cm (2in) pieces of flax (from craft shops and garden centres) or hairy string for beard
50cm (20in) length narrow piping cord or string for ties
Wooden bead 2.5cm (1in) diameter
Mini basket 7–10cm (3–4in) wide
Dried moss to line basket
Small twig
Packet of wallpaper paste
Scissors
Baking sheet
Sticky tape
Household glue
Can of bronze spray paint
Opened out polythene bag, for working on so protecting work surface

Cut an oblong of card 20cm (8in) high x 26cm (10in). Roll this up into a cone shape and fix together with sticky tape. Make a hole at each side at the top of the cone, 2.5cm (1in) from top pointed edge.

Twist two pipe cleaners together at one end, make a loop in a third approximately 4cm (1¹/2in) deep and join to the other pipe cleaners at the middle by twisting together. This forms the head, neck and arm pieces. Insert this in the top of the cone; pull the arms from the inside to the outside through the holes and bend back the ends into loops to form hands. Trim the base of the cone so that it will stand up on its own.

Insert a small ball of cotton wool into the middle of the head loop, and a tiny piece in each of the two hand loops. Mix up half the packet of wallpaper paste to a thick creamy consistency, following manufacturer's instructions. Tear strips of tissue into 12mm (¹/2in) x 20cm (8in) lengths, dip a length into the paste and coat well. Wrap this around the head piece, enclosing the cotton wool, and mould an oval face shape between your thumb and forefingers, adding further strips of tissue in the same way. Smooth out any creases as you go. Pinch in the centre of face to form a nose for Joseph. Wrap tissue in same way for the neck and hands, bend arms to required positions before wrapping the arm pieces. The figure is now ready to be clothed, and the following stages should be worked on a polythene sheet to avoid sticking to work surface.

Take a strip of fabric 40cm (15in) wide x 25cm (10in) deep, and make two slits in the middle of it 3cm (1¹/4in) from top edge and the same width apart as the arms. Mix up the remainder of the paste and dip strip of fabric into it, squeeze out excess glue; carefully insert the arms of the figure through the slits and wrap fabric around the body, overlap fabric at back and stick together. For Mary, add some tissue under the robe fabric to make fuller. Turn under 6mm (¹/4in) at top edge and 12mm (¹/2in) at bottom edge to neaten, then press fabric together into small folds to resemble pleats and drapes. As the fabric is longer than the body, curve the fabric out at the base; this will help in supporting the figure. For the sleeves, take a 20cm (8in)-sided triangle of fabric, dip in paste and fold inwards a hem of 2.5cm (1in). Lay this over the middle of the arm; point of triangle should come at top of arm. Wrap fabric loosely around the arm and glue together by overlapping on the underside.

For Mary's hair, cut five pieces of string 18cm (7in) long and unravel to give a crinkled effect; glue the middle of these strands to the top of the head. For Joseph's beard and moustache cut lengths of flax and glue in position on the face. Make veils for both Mary and Joseph by cutting two triangles of fabric, 25cm (10in) each side. Dip

NATIVITY SCENE

each in paste, fold 2.5cm (1in) under along one edge and drape over head, making folds as before. Tie a length of cord around Joseph's waist, and a shorter length around his head, securing the veil. Stand figures on a baking sheet and dry in a preheated oven 100°C/200°F, gas mark $1/4$ for ten minutes (with non-fan-assisted ovens, leave door slightly open for steam to evaporate). An airing cupboard would also dry the figures, over a longer period of time. When completely dry, spray figures all over with bronze paint and leave to dry.

To make the baby Jesus, fix the bead onto a pipe-cleaner with glue. Fold the wire in half and wrap some cotton wool around for the body. Cut a triangle of fabric, each side 13cm (5in) long, dip this in paste and turn one edge under; with this edge at the top wrap around the ball, under the chin and around the body and tuck under at the bottom. Dry as before, and spray with paint.

Line basket with moss, and lay baby in it. Arrange figures in a family group, put a small twig in Joseph's hand for a crook.

Other figures for the crib can be made by following the same principles. If you want a figure to be kneeling, make a shorter cone. To make animals, twist pipe cleaners to form head, body and legs, pad with cotton wool and wrap tissue around as before. Dry and paint as required.

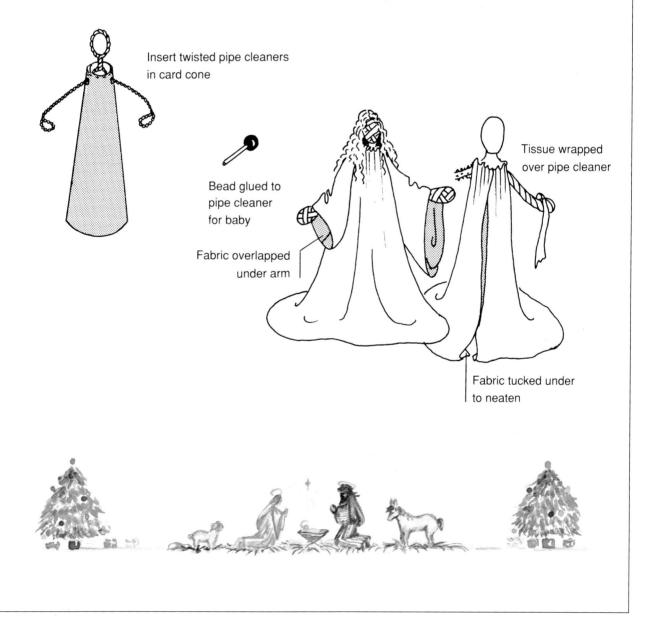

Insert twisted pipe cleaners in card cone

Bead glued to pipe cleaner for baby

Fabric overlapped under arm

Tissue wrapped over pipe cleaner

Fabric tucked under to neaten

CHAPTER THREE

CARDS AND GIFT WRAPPINGS

COVERED AND LINED BOXES

*T*he uses for these attractive boxes are *endless. The same method is used for all shapes and sizes. Experiment with fabric and wallpaper – you will be delighted with the results.*

MATERIALS

Sheet of A2 59cm x 41cm (23³/₈in x 16¹/₂in)
white card
Scissors
Glue and spraymount adhesive
Double-sided sticky tape
Sheet of wrapping paper or wallpaper or fabric
50cm (20in) x 90cm (36in) wide
Polyester wadding 1cm (¹/₂in) thick to fit lid size
Tracing paper
Skewer
Approximately 20cm (8in) piping cord for handles
Ideas for trims: Piping cord, ric rac, ribbon, lace, broderie anglaise, furnishing trims, artificial flowers, tassels, pearl beading, embroidered motifs. Quantities needed are gauged from the circumference of the box.

Grade the box patterns to required size, trace onto the card and cut out. To grade the pattern: for a circular box use a compass to draw a larger or smaller circle, remembering the lid needs to be approximately 12mm (¹/₂in) larger than its base. For the heart-shaped box see Techniques. Cut two strips of card: one 4cm (1¹/₂in) deep x circumference of the lid plus 2cm (³/₄in) overlap and the other 13cm (5in) deep x circumference of the base plus overlap. (NB On both patterns, outer line is lid outline, inner line is base outline.) If you wish to have a padded lid, cut lid shape out of wadding and glue to top of card lid.

Cut two lids in paper or fabric, allowing 12mm (¹/₂in) turning on outer lid piece. Spray glue on the wrong side of the lid piece of fabric and lay over the wadding. Snip into the fabric at 12mm (¹/₂in) intervals around the circumference up to the edge of the card; fold the snipped pieces under the lid, sticking down firmly as you go to secure fabric to card. Glue the remaining lid section to the underside of the wadded lid piece, keeping edges of fabric flush to the lid edge and hiding the turned back edges.

Using the strips of card as your measuring guide, lay the card on a folded piece of fabric, top edge of card flush with the fold. Cut out a fabric length that is 2.5cm (1in) larger than the card on

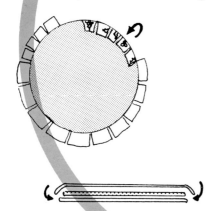

Snip and fold fabric to wrong side

Fold fabric down over wadding for padded lid

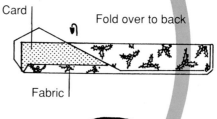

Card

Fold over to back

Fabric

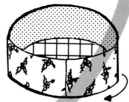

Wrap fabric around base

COVERED AND LINED BOXES

the three edges to allow for turnings. Spray glue onto the wrong side of the fabric strip, lay the card along the strip in the centre of the fabric. Fold the fabric over from the underside of the card as diagram, along lower edge and stick down; then fold the extended fabric piece down over the turned up edge and trim fabric flush to the lower edge. Mitre the corners of the extensions and then bond them together to form a ring. These rings form the sides and rim of lid and base pieces.

Glue inside unfolded edge of narrow strip to outer edge of lid and inside unfolded edge of deeper strip to base edge, overlap the ends and glue down. To secure lid and base to sides of box, add some glue all around on the inside edges.

Decorate with any of the above trim ideas. Rough edges can be concealed with cord, ribbon or lace trims. To make handles for a box, pierce through all thicknesses with a skewer, push required length of piping cord through to the inside and knot the ends. Omit the wadding in the lid if you require a flat surface.

CHRISTMAS CHAPEAU

Make this delightful hat to camouflage a small gift. The crown can be opened where it meets the brim; open up with a sharp knife by slitting the sticky tape on the inside of the crown, allowing the gift to be removed. The crown can be restuck to the brim turning the hat into a wall decoration.

MATERIALS

A2 59cm x 41cm (23³/8in x 16¹/2in) piece red cartridge paper
1 round cheese box base approximately 11cm (4¹/4in) diameter
Sheet of lightweight card
Glue
64cm (25in) red braid 6mm (¹/4in) wide
1m (40in) scalloped-edged lace 2.5cm (1in) wide
38cm (15in) red tartan ribbon 2cm (³/4in) wide
64cm (24in) red tartan ribbon 4cm (1¹/2in) wide
Double-sided sticky tape

Draw around the base of the box onto the red paper, cut out a circle and glue this on the base. Cut a strip of red paper 38cm (15in) x 3cm (1¹/4in) and glue around the side of the box, overlapping the ends. Glue the narrow ribbon around the side of the box base.

Cut three circles, two in red paper and one in card, 18cm (7¹/4in) in diameter (approximately the size of a side plate). Glue the red braid around the outer edge of one red circle, gather lace with small running stitches and glue it to the underside of the same circle. Glue the other red circle to the card circle and then to the underside of the trimmed circle (with the card circle 'sandwiched') to neaten and form the hat brim.

Cut 4cm (1¹/2in) strips of double-sided tape and stick at 4cm (1¹/2in) intervals around the inside of the upturned box base, enclose gift and stick crown of hat to the brim base. Make a big bow out of the wide ribbon and glue in position at centre back.

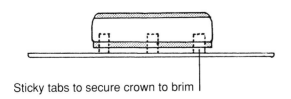

Sticky tabs to secure crown to brim

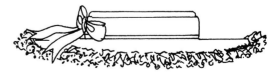

Add lace and bow to complete

DINNER-JACKET BOX

This is a clever way to disguise the usual pair of socks or a tie that most men have come to rely on receiving at Christmas!

MATERIALS

Oblong carton 25cm (10in) x 17cm (6^1/$_2$in) x 4cm (1^1/$_2$in)
A4 29^1/$_2$cm x 21cm (11^3/$_4$in x 8^1/$_4$in) sheet white cartridge paper
A2 59cm x 41cm (23^3/$_8$in x 16^1/$_2$in) sheet black cartridge paper
30cm (12in) x 3cm (1^1/$_4$in) red tartan ribbon
10cm (4in) square of white cotton fabric
2 small white buttons
Double-sided sticky tape
Glue
86cm (34in) gold cord braid
Tracing paper

Fold black paper over the box and anchor with double-sided tape. Make a lapel in black paper and cut out; reverse this and cut out for other side. Glue a strip of gold braid on the under-edge of each lapel, ensuring that the braid fits neatly into the curves.

Lay lapels on the covered box overlapping them at the lower edge, draw in lightly the V shape they make on the box. Remove the lapels and cut a triangle of white paper to fit the V allowing some extra to come under the lapels, so covering up the black paper and giving the appearance of a shirt under the jacket. Make a slit as marked on diagram and crease back to form the collar wings. Glue a smaller piece of white paper to the underside of the white V piece, thus filling in the triangular neck piece left after folding back the collar section. Glue the white triangular piece in the middle of the flat surface of the covered box; next glue a lapel on the left side, slightly overlapping the edge of the white paper. Position the right lapel over the left at the bottom and glue in place, to resemble a jacket front.

Cut a small strip of black paper 5cm (2in) x 2cm (^{3}/$_4$in), and a triangle of white fabric 10cm (4in) each side. Fold the white fabric to hide raw edges, stick it to the back of the black pocket strip to form a handkerchief, and glue in position on the right side of the jacket.

Make a bow for the tie from the tartan ribbon and glue this under the wing collar. To complete, glue on the two buttons to the shirt as marked.

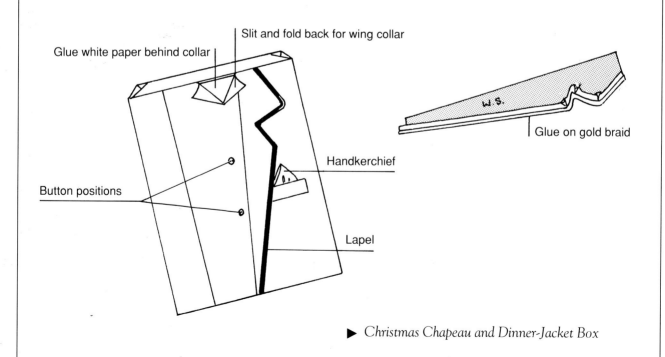

► *Christmas Chapeau and Dinner-Jacket Box*

WRAPPING PAPER

*W*ith the price of paper today, it makes *sound sense to print your own for a fraction of the cost. The initial outlay for some methods may appear expensive, but you will be able to print a lot of paper for your money. Our easy ideas have their own individual qualities – you can even get the children to join in the fun of making their own paper.*

MATERIALS
Lino

Oddment of lino
Lino-cutting tools
Ink roller
Water-based printing inks
Tracing paper
Newspaper
25cm (10in) square glass oddment for ink and roller

Stencil

20cm (8in) square of stencil parchment
Tube of picture framer's gold paste
Turpentine
Stencil brush and stiff paintbrush
Fixative spray

Potato

Potato
Felt pen
Sharp knife
Kitchen paper towel
Powder paints

Suggestions for pattern repeats

Paper for printing: this will depend on the end use and final effect you wish to create. You can use inexpensive sugar paper, brown paper, tissue paper, cartridge paper etc. Lining paper for walls is an economical way to produce a long run of the same design, often a requirement for those large presents!

LINO

Trace the design onto the lino. It is easier to cut out your design if the surface of the lino has been warmed first. Working on a doubled piece of newspaper, use a narrow blade in your lino tool to mark the outline of the design, remembering that the raised lino left forms the pattern which is printed. The more slowly you work the better. For the removal of larger areas use a broader tool; take great care not to cut your fingers. The deeper you make your cuts the cleaner the print will be, but the tool marks add dimension to a print so do not worry if you leave some. Shake off excess pieces and wipe with a damp cloth before printing.

Squeeze some ink onto the glass and evenly cover the roller with the ink before rolling over the cut side of the lino. Roll in a forwards/backwards and side-to-side motion so that the design is well covered. Lay lino face down in position on the paper to be printed, and press down firmly. Carefully turn over so that paper is on top, and rub over the paper with a clean rag. Do this a few times, checking that the outline is clear; when lino becomes too inky, wash it with soapy water. Repeat the printing process as many times as required; you can choose an all-over print or space the design in a patchwork effect.

STENCIL

Make the stencil using the same method as for the Christmas Tree Mat on page 34. Stipple the design using the stencil brush. The gold paste is oil-based, so you will need turpentine to clean the stencil after printing. To ensure that the finely cut areas are covered, use a stiff paintbrush to get right into the corners. After printing the design spray it with fixative to secure. As the gold paste is expensive, wrap your present first and print it

WRAPPING PAPER

afterwards to save any wasted paper. Make your own gift tags or printed ribbons following the same method.

POTATO

Potato printing is great fun for children; the principles are the same as for lino. Your designs have to be simple: Cut a potato in half, outline your design on the flat surface with a felt pen, then cut away area around the line with a sharp knife. The remaining raised area is that which will be printed.

When the potato is ready for printing wipe off excess juice with a paper towel, dip the design in the mixed powder paint and print as required. Wash the potato after a few prints.

There are many other ideas to consider, such as making a design with a glue pen and then agitating some glitter onto it, shaking when dry to remove excess. If you do not want to print your wrapping paper, you can achieve a similar effect by using coloured gummed paper cut-out shapes, or Victorian paper scraps, stuck on a sheet of paper. A money saving idea, if your parcel has flat surfaces, is to wrap the gift first and stick on the paper shapes afterwards. This also applies to the stencil ideas, saving on paint and gold paste.

Lino motif

Stencil motif

Glue on pompon if used

Cut away solid lines with fine lino blade

Lino motif

Actual size

Stencil motif

GREETINGS CARDS

There are a variety of ways in which you can make your Christmas greetings cards. Depending on your skills, our selection will ring the changes. All will be well received and the handiwork much admired.

FELT-TRIMMED CARDS

MATERIALS

Blank mount card and envelope
Scraps of felt in colours as follows:
10cm (4in) square of brown felt for the pudding
White felt 10cm (4in) wide x 5cm (2in) deep for the icing
Gold felt 10cm (4in) long x 2cm (^{3}/4in) wide for the plate
Scraps of black felt for currants, red for berries, green for holly
Glue
Tracing paper

Trace the design and cut out in appropriate coloured felt. Stick onto the folded card following the design layout.

WINE BOTTLE IN TOTE BAG

MATERIALS

1 doll's-house-size wine bottle
10cm (4in) square of gold wrapping paper
5cm (2in) square of tissue paper
2 x 8cm (3^1/4in) lengths of ribbon 2mm (^{1}/8in) wide
Former (long narrow matchbox) 5cm x 2.5cm (2in x 1in)
Hole punch
Glue
Holly trim
Mounting card and envelope
(Holly trim and doll's-house-size wine bottles can be bought from specialist doll's-house shops.)

Make a tiny carrier bag as for the tote bag method on page 61. Pack some tissue paper into the base of the bag, glue the bottle in the top of the bag and add some holly trim. Fold card in half and glue the bag to it in the centre.

Glue bag to front of folded card

Wine bottle in Tote Bag

Glue on felt cut-outs

Felt-trimmed Cards

Machine-stitch outline

Sew on star bead

Wadding

Mary and Baby Jesus

GREETINGS CARDS

MARY AND BABY JESUS

MATERIALS

2 x 30cm (12in) squares of beige cotton fabric
30cm (12in) square polyester wadding 1cm
(1/2in) thick
Tracing paper
Fixative spray
Watercolour paints and brush
Diamond trim for star
Pale blue card picture mount with oval cut out
25cm (10in) x 20cm (8in) and envelope to fit
Glue and sticky tape

Trace the design onto one fabric square; lay this on top of the wadding square with remaining fabric square underneath, thus sandwiching wadding between fabrics. Machine around the pencil outlines through all thicknesses. Spray top side with fixative, and when dry paint the face and hands in relevant facial and eye colours. Sew on star. Mount work in card mount, attaching it with sticky tape to the back of the card, and glue a piece of card, the same size as the mount when folded, to the back, to make a stand-up card.

CROSS-STITCH BELL

MATERIALS

Ready-made card with bell-shaped mount
Square Zweigart Aida 14 holes to 2.5cm (1in) to
fit mount
Stranded embroidery cotton in shades shown on
the key
Glue
Small ribbon bow

Outline bell shape from card onto paper for use as a guide for working your cross stitch. Follow the chart, extending stitching beyond the template to ensure your work comes underneath the mount. Glue finished work to underside of card mount. Finish with a bow glued to top of bell.

Diamond trim star

Paint in face, neck and hand features

Machine-quilt along solid lines

Actual size

DMC		ANCHOR
904	▨	258
832	·	890

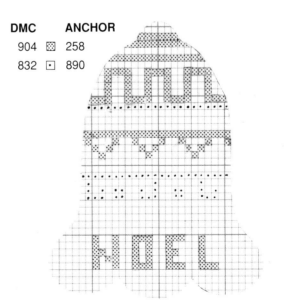

The chart is 23 stitches wide by 34 stitches deep

SEASONAL GREETINGS IN NEEDLEPOINT

Make this richly embroidered Christmas card for someone special. It is a real labour of love that will be treasured for years, and would look good in an antique frame brought out each Christmas. Finished design measures 14cm (5¹/₂in) x 20cm (8in)

MATERIALS

Stranded embroidery cotton in shades detailed on colour key

30cm (12in) square of Zweigart single thread canvas, with 18 holes to 2.5cm (1in)

Tapestry needle size 20

Card for mounting, approximately 19cm (7¹/₂in) x 26cm (10¹/₂in)

Craft knife, metal ruler, emery board

Backing card in white for tapestry, approximately 13cm (5¹/₄in) x 19.5cm (7³/₄in)

Masking tape, glue

The needlepoint can be worked in the hand, or stretched onto a frame. Fold the canvas in half and then again in quarters and mark the centre with small tacking stitches top to bottom and side to side. Use masking tape to bind raw side edges of canvas to prevent yarn from snagging. Stretch canvas onto a frame by stitching each end of the canvas to the webbing strips with small stitches using needle and double cotton thread. Roll the stitched rods over at the top and bottom and secure the fly bolts to make work taut for stitching. Follow the chart opposite. See stitch guide in Techniques for method. Each square represents one tent stitch on the canvas.

Working from the centre of the canvas, start with darkest colours first to keep the work clean; use six strands of cotton in the needle throughout.

When the design is completed, it may need stretching into shape. Carefully pull diagonally in each corner, then press your work gently on the reverse side with an iron and damp cloth. Trim edges of finished work, then stretch needlepoint over the card and catch the back together with long stitches from one side of the canvas to the other, using six threads of stranded cotton in your needle and pulling the work taut as you stitch down.

MOUNTING THE CARD

Cut card to size using a sharp craft knife and cut out a window mount in the middle of the card to fit the outer edges of the work. To ensure neat edges around the card edge, smooth with an emery board. Secure the needlepoint with masking tape on the wrong side of the card, with right side of work facing upwards.

Fold white card in half to same size as outer edges of the mount. Glue the mount onto the front of the folded card. Write your greetings with transfer lettering or italic script in pen and ink.

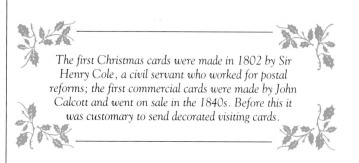

The first Christmas cards were made in 1802 by Sir Henry Cole, a civil servant who worked for postal reforms; the first commercial cards were made by John Calcott and went on sale in the 1840s. Before this it was customary to send decorated visiting cards.

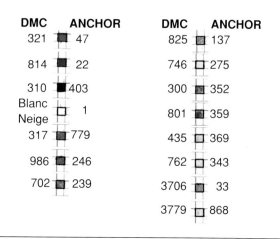

DMC		ANCHOR	DMC		ANCHOR
321	■	47	825	▨	137
814	■	22	746	□	275
310	■	403	300	▨	352
Blanc Neige	□	1	801	■	359
317	▨	779	435	□	369
986	■	246	762	□	343
702	▨	239	3706	▨	33
			3779	□	868

The chart is 90 stitches wide by 136 stitches deep

TOTE BAGS

Make these simple bags as large or as small as you like to wrap those awkward presents. Use either bought paper, or your own printed paper co-ordinated with a matching card.

MATERIALS

Sheets of wrapping paper
Double-sided sticky tape
1m (40in) cord/ribbon
Hole punch
Boxes or pile of books as formers
Card (for weighty gifts)

Select some books of equal size or boxes that are bigger than the gift to be wrapped.

Fold over 3cm (1¹/4in) to the wrong side on the top edge of the wrapping paper. With right side of the paper face down, lay the books in the middle of it; wrap the paper around the former and join the overlapping long edges with double-sided tape. Fold the paper at the bottom edge into triangular flaps as for a parcel and stick the top flap on the underside over the lower flap using double-sided sticky tape. Run a thumbnail along the edges of the former to give a keen edge. Slide the former out of the bag at the top open edge, easing it out and under the inside folded edge. Make two holes with the hole punch in the middle of the folded edge approximately 5cm (2in) apart.

Cut two lengths of cord or ribbon for handles: pass through the holes from the right side and knot ends on the inside of the bag. Make an invert pleat at each side of the bag by creasing down the length of the side panels in the middle. Some heavier gifts may need extra support at the base; for this, cut a strip of card to fit in the base of the bag. Add optional trims such as ribbon roses, dried flowers or Christmas decorations to complete.

◀ *Seasonal Greetings in Needlepoint*

CARD GIFT BOX AND ENVELOPE

These provide excellent protection for small gifts. Choose an unusual trim for that extra-special personal touch.

MATERIALS

A2 59cm x 41cm (23³/₈in x 16¹/₂in) sheet
foil-backed card
Tracing paper
Tissue paper
Glue
Ruler, compass, scissors, blunt knife
Trim ideas: ribbon, bought bells, dried flowers and
mini ornaments

Grade the pattern opposite (see Techniques) and outline onto the card. Cut out and score along the fold lines using a ruler and blunt knife. Bend all folding sections as in diagram, and glue together marked flaps.

For the envelope, draw the curve with a compass, and score around a curved edge such as a saucer. Insert gift wrapped in tissue and decorate with trims of your choice.

For larger or smaller boxes, grade the patterns to the required size (see Techniques). Small gift envelopes and boxes made from lightweight printed card and filled with chocolate buttons or gifts would make pretty tree ornaments.

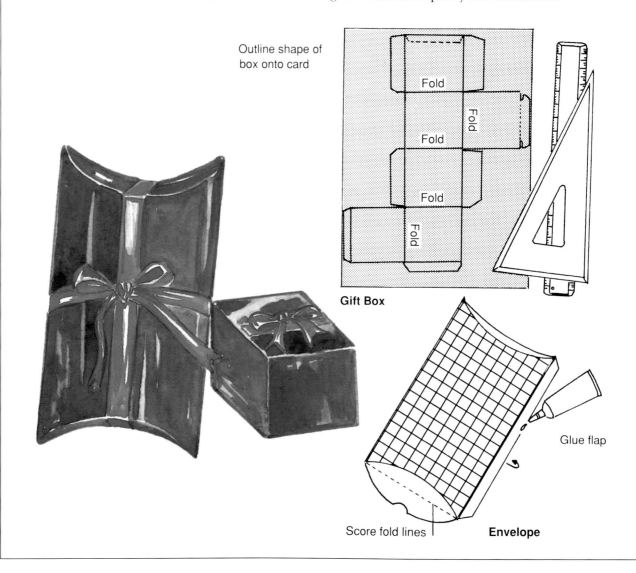

Outline shape of box onto card

Fold
Fold
Fold
Fold
Fold

Gift Box

Glue flap

Score fold lines

Envelope

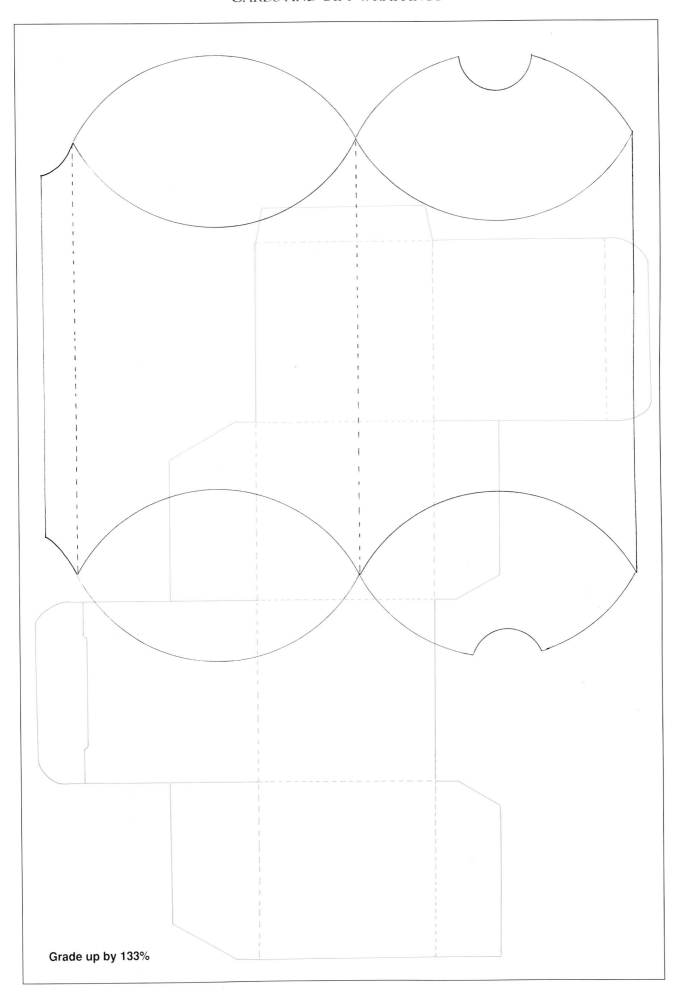

Grade up by 133%

CHAPTER FOUR

A Feast from the Pantry

DECORATED HAMPER BASKET

*T*his basket would make a wonderful gift filled with a selection of homemade goodies. By changing the printed fabric you could turn it into a summer picnic basket – choose a tempting strawberry print to get you in the mood for those balmy days to come.

MATERIALS

Basket with opening lids (ours measures 51cm (20in) long x 38cm (15in) wide x 23cm (9in) deep)

1m (40in) cotton print fabric 140cm (54in) wide

4m (160in) satin bias binding 12mm (^{1}/2in) wide

3m (120in) elastic 6mm (^{1}/4in) wide

1m (40in) satin ribbon 7cm (3in) wide

6m (240in) cotton dressmaker's tape 12mm (^{1}/2in) wide

30cm (12in) polyester wadding 140cm (54in) wide

A2 59cm x 41cm (23^3/8in x 16^1/2in) sheet card

Outline the lids of your basket onto card. They will need copying individually as handmade baskets are rarely symmetrical. Use the card template to cut out two of each lid in fabric and one of each in wadding. Cut a strip of binding to fit across the top edge of the fabric lids. Sandwich the wadding between the material and bind the straight side enclosing the raw edges; machine the binding close to unfolded inner edge.

Cut length of binding to fit around the curved edge, allowing 40cm (16in) at each side of lid for ties. With binding folded, start on left side of lid and pin around curved edge enclosing all thicknesses, and machine-stitch on close to inner edge. Knot raw ends of ties. Press with an iron and tie

on top of the basket lids with a bow each side of the handle.

To make the frill, cut two lengths of cotton fabric each totalling twice the circumference of the basket rim and deep enough to fold over the rim edge with some to spare for a frill. Our basket needs two 152cm (60in) x 24cm (9^1/2in) strips. Turn up and machine a 6mm (^{1}/4in) hem all the way around the strip. Make two channels with the tape to enclose the elastic: these need to be 7.5cm (3in) apart and centred along the length of each strip. Leave ends open and insert the elastic, then draw up elastic to the half measurement of the basket rim and secure ends with small stitches.

Lay the middle of gathered frill over the edge of the basket, space frills evenly on inside and outside. Stitch in position by sewing through the basket from outside to inside, catching the gathers on both sides.

To complete, tie a big satin bow around the handle in the middle. Catch the sides of the frills together with small stitches.

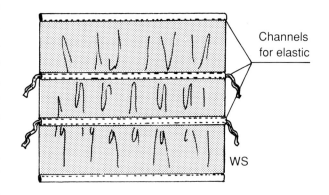

Channels for elastic

WS

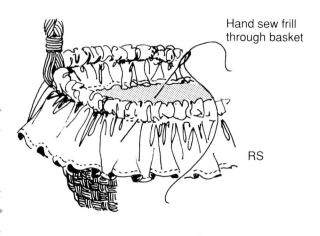

Hand sew frill through basket

RS

Centuries ago salmon was the traditional fare for Christmas lunch. William Strickland introduced the turkey, a native of Mexico and North America, to England in the 1500s. Turkeys became so popular in George II's reign that he kept a flock in Richmond Park.

GINGERBREAD COTTAGE

*T*his delightful cottage should attract children today, as much as the one in the memorable story of Hansel and Gretel attracted our grandparents. The decoration is something the family will love to join in with; that is, if they can resist eating the sweets first!

INGREDIENTS

For the cake

240g (9^1/$_2$oz) brown sugar
300g (12oz) honey
500g (1lb 2oz) margarine
200ml (8fl oz/1 cup) orange juice
1.2kg (2lb 10oz) wholemeal flour
3tsp bicarbonate of soda
3tsp cinnamon and ginger
^{1}/$_2$tsp white pepper
2 size 4 eggs
A2 59cm x 41cm (23^3/$_8$in x 16^1/$_2$in) sheet card
Baking sheet

For assembly and decoration

3 egg whites
1tsp lemon juice
350g (12^1/$_2$oz) icing sugar
1 cup of granulated sugar
Teddy bear jelly sweets
Red, green and white candy-coated chocolate buttons
Liquorice Allsorts
Sprigs of evergreen for fir trees

TO MAKE THE COTTAGE

Weigh and sieve the flour into a large bowl, add spices and soda. Melt the sugar, margarine and honey in a saucepan, allow to bubble well to dissolve the ingredients. When cool add the orange juice and beaten eggs, add to the flour and knead the dough with your knuckles. Cover the dough in a bowl and leave in the refrigerator overnight.

Transfer the shapes of the cottage onto card following the diagram. Cut out and use as templates. You will need to cut out two of each piece in the dough, plus one door and one base for the cottage to stand on.

Divide the dough into three. Roll out one third to 12mm (¹/₂in) thick. Onto this, trace around the card for the front and side panels, gently outlining them in the dough with the point of a sharp knife. Lay the section on a flat baking sheet, prick all over with a fork and glaze with a solution of honey and water. Repeat for the other side and back pieces in the second piece of dough.

Cook in a preheated oven at 200°C/400°F, gas mark 6, for ten to fifteen minutes, ensuring the edges do not burn. When cooked, cut out the shapes in the dough while still warm, then leave on a wire rack to cool. Roll out the third piece of dough and mark the two roof sections, and a random oval to form the base for the cottage to stand on. With some of the scraps make a fence and door. Cook and cut as above.

ASSEMBLING AND DECORATING THE COTTAGE

Melt granulated sugar in a saucepan (a small quantity at a time as it goes hard very quickly) and use this as 'glue' for attaching front, sides and edges of the cottage to each other and to the base. The sections will need to be propped up with a weighted object whilst they stick together. The joints can be secured further with some icing. When all sections are bonded, the roof pieces can be fixed in position with the melted sugar.

Sift the icing sugar and add the egg and lemon juice, stir to a dropping consistency. Spread this over the top of the roof and allow it to run over the edges, forming icicles. Gently press the candy buttons in rows onto the roof, resembling tiles. Fix Liquorice Allsorts to the gable ends and along the top of the roof with dabs of icing.

SAFETY FIRST: *Keep the heated and melted sugar well out of reach of children, as it can burn skin on contact.*

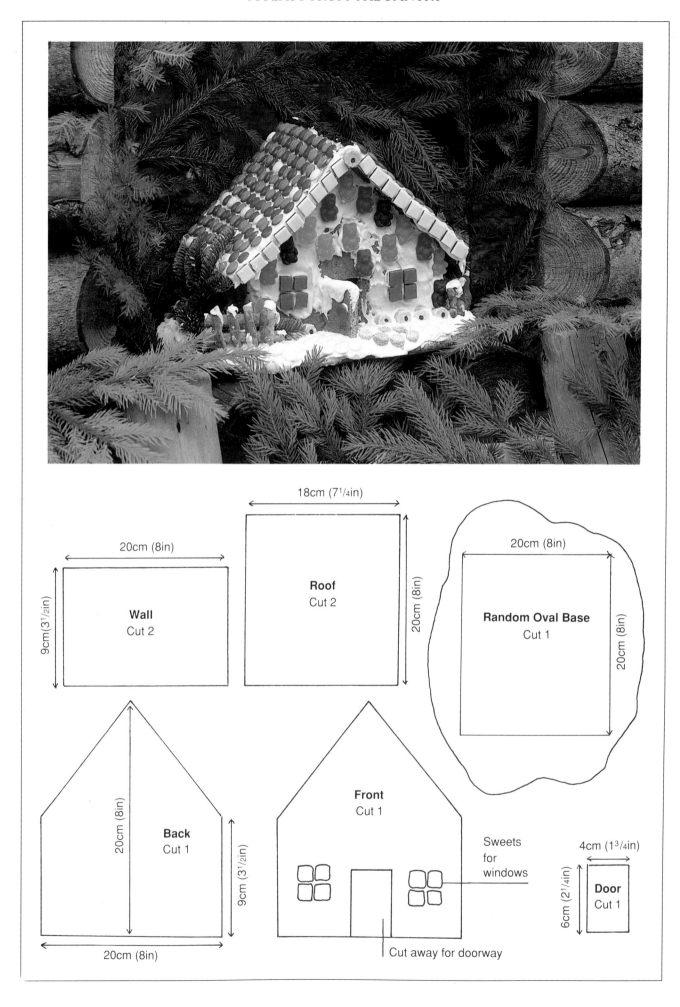

18cm (7¼in)

Roof
Cut 2

20cm (8in)

20cm (8in)

Wall
Cut 2

9cm(3½in)

20cm (8in)

Random Oval Base
Cut 1

20cm (8in)

Back
Cut 1

20cm (8in)

9cm (3½in)

20cm (8in)

Front
Cut 1

Sweets
for
windows

Cut away for doorway

4cm (1¾in)

Door
Cut 1

6cm (2¼in)

GINGERBREAD COTTAGE

Thinly cover the top half of the front section with icing and embed jelly teddy bears and brown Allsorts for windows. Attach the door to the front with icing and add a red button for the door knob. Spread icing over base, around the sides and in front of the cottage, fix the fence each side at the front. Finally, add some stems of pine to give the effect of a forest.

Tip: With leftover pieces make some gingerbread figures or star- and heart-shaped biscuits. Ice and decorate with silver balls, and make a hole in the top to thread a piece of ribbon through so these can be hung on the Christmas tree.

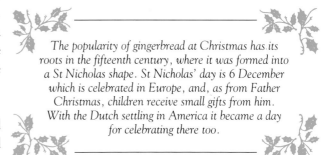

The popularity of gingerbread at Christmas has its roots in the fifteenth century, where it was formed into a St Nicholas shape. St Nicholas' day is 6 December which is celebrated in Europe, and, as from Father Christmas, children receive small gifts from him. With the Dutch settling in America it became a day for celebrating there too.

VICTORIAN PLUM PUDDING

Make this fruity Christmas pudding in the traditional round shape to add nostalgia to the festive table. Wrapped in a cheerful gingham cloth it would make a welcome gift.

INGREDIENTS

350g (12oz) soft white breadcrumbs
675g (1¹/2lb) raisins
225g (¹/2lb) currants
225g (¹/2lb) mixed peel
100g (4oz) soft brown sugar
350g (³/4lb) shredded suet
2.5ml (¹/2 level tsp) each of mixed spice,
cinnamon, nutmeg
4 size 4 eggs
30ml (2tbsp/US 3tbsp) treacle
150ml (¹/4pt/²/3 cup) dark rum
Icing sugar for dusting
Lucky charm or coin
50cm (20in) piece of string
50cm (20in) piece of ribbon 2.5cm (1in) wide
80cm (30in) piece each of gingham and muslin,
90cm (36in) wide

Mix all the dry ingredients in a bowl, whisk eggs and stir into the mixture gradually. Slowly add the rum and treacle and mix well. Add your charm or coin and make a wish.

Flour the muslin cloth well before putting the dough in the centre of it. Shape the mixture into a ball, draw up the muslin tightly and tie at the top with string. Cook in steamer over boiling water for six hours. When cool, wrap in gingham cloth and tie with ribbon bow and holly.

When required for eating, remove from the gingham and boil the pudding in the muslin for two hours. Remove from muslin and sprinkle icing sugar over the top. Serve on a warmed plate with flaming brandy, accompanied by brandy butter and cream.

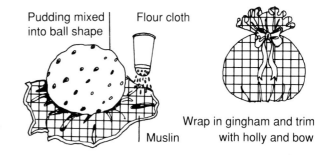

Pudding mixed into ball shape | Flour cloth

Muslin

Wrap in gingham and trim with holly and bow

JAMPOT COVERS AND LABELS

*I*f you need to create a gift in a hurry, then these ideas are simple but effective. It is a good idea to have some extras to hand, for those unexpected callers. Quantities below are for a lid cover size 8cm (3in) in diameter, and a label to fit a jar 23cm (9in) in circumference.

MATERIALS

Covers:

20cm (8in) cotton fabric
Approximately 20cm (8in) shirring elastic
50cm (20in) bias binding
Pinking shears
1m (40in) ribbon 12mm (^{1}/2in) wide
2m (80in) ribbon 3mm (^{1}/8in) wide

Variations:

Ready-made crochet mat approximately 23cm (9in) in diameter
20cm (8in) square Zweigart Aida cloth 14 holes per 2.5cm (1in) for one cover
Fabric pens

Labels:

15cm (6in) x 9cm (3^1/2in) Zweigart Aida cloth 14 holes per 2.5cm (1in) for one label
Stranded embroidery cotton in shades detailed on colour key

Approximately 50cm (20in) 1cm (^{1}/2in) wide bias binding for each label
Approximately 50cm (20in) 3mm (^{1}/8in) wide ribbon

COVERS

Draw a circle around a side plate on a piece of fabric and cut out with pinking shears.

Thread the bobbin with the elastic and machine around the circle 3cm (1^1/4in) in from pinked edge, gathering as you stitch. Glue a ribbon bow on right side of machined line.

VARIATIONS

• Crochet a cover, or use a bought mat, thread a ribbon in and out 3cm (1^1/4in) in from edge then draw it up, tying a knot and finishing off with a bow on the jamjar.
• Bind a circle of plain fabric with bias binding, elasticate as above and draw a design on the top with fabric pens.
• Cut a circle of Aida cloth, elasticate as above and bind the edges and work the strawberry motif on the top.

LABELS

Work the designs from the chart in the book on some scraps of Zweigart Aida fabric, neaten the raw edges with bias binding and sew on ribbons at each side for attaching to the jar.

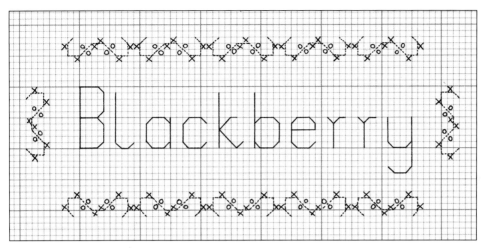

The chart is 72 stitches wide by 28 stitches deep

The chart is 54 stitches wide by 34 stitches deep

Blackberry

	DMC		ANCHOR
Backstitch	552	—	100
Backstitch	986	---	246
Cross stitch	3347	×	261
French knots	552	o	100

Strawberry

	DMC		ANCHOR
	986	▧	246
	746	▨	386
	666	▨	334
Backstitch	666	—	334
Backstitch outline	310	—	403
French knots	726	✿	297

Strawberry and Blackberry Brooches

Strawberry

You will need four pieces of red spotted fabric approximately 7.5cm (3in) square for the strawberry, a handful of polyester wadding, a scrap of green felt, brooch pin and two small white artificial flowers.

Cut out four 5cm (2in) deep heart shapes in the fabric. Machine around the edge on the wrong side of each pair of shapes, leaving a small opening for turning to the right side. Snip up to the seamline, turn to the right side and wad with the polyester. Sew up the opening.

Cut 2 small star shapes approximately 2.5cm (1in) in diameter for the calyces in the felt, glue these to the tops of the fruits with the flowers. Cut two stems in the felt and sew to the fruits. Sew stems together at the top, joining the two fruits together. Glue or sew to the brooch pin.

Blackberry

You will need two small artificial flowers, one packet of tiny blackberry-coloured glass beads, cotton wool ball, two 10cm (4in) wire stems, 15cm (6in) square of organza, scrap of green felt, cotton thread and a brooch pin.

Wrap some cotton wool around the wire the size of a blackberry, drape over an 8cm (3in) piece of organza and secure with some cotton thread twisted around the base of the bundle. Sew the beads around the pad, covering it up to resemble a blackberry fruit. Trim away excess organza fabric at the base of the fruit. Repeat the method for another fruit, wire the two together and finish off as for the strawberry.

Pin the brooches to the top of the pot covers.

DECORATED BOTTLES AND JARS

*R*evive the tastes of summer with delicious *preserves, mouthwatering jams and herby vinegars presented in finely decorated bottles and jars.*

MATERIALS

Glass bottles and jars in a variety of shapes and sizes
Glass paints and brush
Carbon paper
Turpentine

Note: You can buy bottles with three-dimensional relief patterns; these look especially good when painted.

Trace your chosen design from page 73, lay this sheet over a sheet of carbon paper with the carbon side face down and trace over outline onto jar or bottle.

Carefully paint in the design with the glass paints, following manufacturer's instructions. When dry, wipe off any remaining carbon with a rag dipped in turpentine.

Tip: Paint a set of plain wine glasses with a small holly design for your Christmas table.

Decorate your Window
Paint a glass disc with the snowflake design opposite in white or silver. Hang it up in your window for a striking effect.

DECORATED BOTTLES AND JARS

Snowflake

Holly Motif

Pine Motif

Cherry Motif

COVERED OVAL SWEET BOX

Make a gift of your marzipan fruits in this unique box – both will be well received and the box can be used afterwards for holding special keepsakes.

MATERIALS

Oval sweet box 18cm (7in) long x 12cm (4^{1}/2in) wide x 10cm (4in) deep
50cm (20in) cotton fabric 90cm (40in) wide
Spray-on glue
50cm (20in) length of tasselled fringe 4cm (1^{1}/2in) deep

Draw around the box lid and the base. Then, with 12mm (^{1}/2in) allowance all around, cut out two lids and two bases in fabric.

Measure depth of box base and cut a strip of fabric 2.5cm (1in) wider and 12mm (^{1}/2in) longer than oval and 12mm (^{1}/2in) deeper than height of base. Do the same for box lid, allowing 12mm (^{1}/2in) width and length for turnings. Cut lining pieces to exact depth of lid and base with 12mm (^{1}/2in) overlaps at ends. Cut lid and base oval lining pieces flush to sides.

Glue and wrap appropriate outer strips around the outside of the lid and base sections, overlapping ends to neaten. Snip up to the edge of the overlaps and fold over the box edge, sticking down firmly. Glue on the outer ovals to neaten the lid and base pieces. Glue the lining strips and lining ovals in position on the inside of the box.

To complete, glue the length of tasselled braid to the bottom edge of the lid.

74

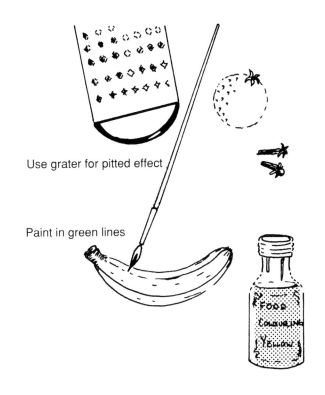

Use grater for pitted effect

Paint in green lines

Dust fruit with caster sugar

Use cloves as stalks

MARZIPAN FRUITS

These delicious candies will be irresistible at your Christmas dinner. They are quick and easy to make so take some as a gift when visiting relations over the Christmas period.

MATERIALS

225g (8oz) white marzipan
Petit-four cases
Cloves
Caster sugar
Food colours: red, green, yellow, blue, orange
Cheese grater

Tip: For luxury versions buy marzipan with added rum, or add your own favourite tipple to liven things up!

Oranges Colour a small amount of the marzipan with orange food colour and work into small balls approximately 2.5cm (1in) diameter. Prick over a cheese grater to give pitted effect. Insert a clove at the top.

Apples Colour a small amount of marzipan green. Work into balls as for oranges. Insert clove at the top.

Strawberries Colour marzipan red, shape as a strawberry, indent on grater for seed effect. Insert clove and dust in caster sugar for frosting.

Bananas Colour some marzipan yellow, roll out and shape as a banana. Paint green colouring along the edges of the fruit.

Grapes Colour the marzipan with some mixed red and blue colouring to give a grape colour, roll into small balls and group together to form a bunch. Insert a clove at the top. Dust in caster sugar.

Leave all fruits to dry before packing.

MRS BUTTER'S SPICED COOKIES

These delicious cookies will be too tempting to keep, so make up some extra dough and store in the freezer. They make fun tree decorations or a tasty present.

INGREDIENTS

350g (12oz) plain flour
100g (4oz) unsalted butter
2 size 4 eggs
200g (7oz) caster sugar
50g (2oz) chopped citrus peel
2.5ml (^{1}/2tsp) ground cardamom
5ml (1 level tsp) ground cinnamon
1.25ml (^{1}/4tsp) ground cloves
5ml (1 level tsp) baking powder
Baking parchment, baking sheet
(Makes approximately 20 cookies)
Toppings White icing: 100g (4oz) sifted icing
sugar mixed with ^{1}/2 egg white
Chocolate covering: 100g (4oz) melted plain
chocolate
Golden glaze: 1 teacup of condensed milk and 1
egg yolk mixed together
Decoration: hundreds-and-thousands, chocolate
vermicelli or crystallised violets.

Sift flour and baking powder into a bowl. Cream together sugar, eggs and spices with 1 tbsp flour to prevent curdling. Finely chop the peel; add peel and half the flour and baking powder to the creamed mixture. Add remaining flour and work to a firm dough with your knuckles. Cover the mixture and leave in the fridge for twenty-four hours.

Preheat the oven to 160°C/325°F, gas mark 3. Line a baking sheet with cooking parchment. Roll out half the dough on a floured work surface to 6mm (^{1}/4in) thick, keeping dough as cool as possible. A marble slab is excellent for this purpose. Cut out cookies using shaped cutters and lay on cooking parchment, well spaced; brush lightly with golden glaze or leave plain if using other toppings listed. Cook in the centre of the oven for approximately fifteen minutes, turn tray halfway through cooking to ensure even browning. When cooked remove to cool on a wire rack. Repeat process with remaining dough.

Cover a third of the cookies with icing, a third with chocolate and a third with glaze. Decorate with trims.

Tip: For tree hanging decoration, make a hole in the cookie with a skewer whilst still warm, thread onto a ribbon when cool.

Punch out biscuit shapes from dough

Tie biscuits on a ribbon for the Christmas tree

FABRIC-COVERED TIN

You can make this in next to no time with a specially chosen new tin, or revitalise your old biscuit and sweet tins. Choose a Christmas print in cotton to add to the festive mood.

MATERIALS

Tea caddy
50cm (20in) cotton fabric 90cm (36in) wide
Spray-on glue
80cm (32in) co-ordinating braid 1cm (¹/2in) wide
20cm (8in) square polyester wadding
1cm (¹/2in) wide

Measure the circumference of the tin and its depth. Then, allowing 12mm (¹/2in) overlap at each end and along sides, cut a strip of fabric to size.

Spray glue on the wrong side of the fabric; place the tin on the glued side and roll fabric around it, tucking in the overlapping ends. Snip the overlapping pieces of fabric at the top and bottom and fold over the edges, press down firmly to secure.

Cut a circle of fabric flush to the edge of the base of the tin, spray glue on the wrong side of fabric and stick to the bottom, covering the overlapping pieces. Measure the diameter of the lid and cut a circle of fabric and wadding to fit the lid of the tin, glue the wadding to the outside and then the fabric on top of the wadding. Cut a narrow strip of fabric to fit the side of the lid and glue around the lid, concealing the edge of the circular lid piece.

To finish off, glue a length of braid around the edge of the tin lid.

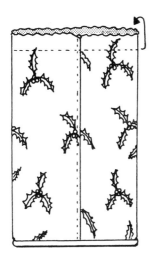

Turn down to inside

Wrap fabric around tin

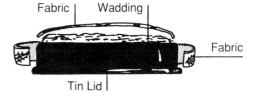

Fabric | Wadding | Fabric

Tin Lid

Glue on braid to neaten

CHAPTER FIVE

DECORATING THE TABLE

POINSETTIA TABLECLOTH, NAPKINS AND RINGS

*T*his seasonal design is easily worked in appliqué and simple embroidery stitches, and the end results will add splendour to any Christmas table. To complete the setting, make the matching napkin rings. To save time you can use ready-made napkins and cloth. Choose whatever shape of cloth suits your table requirement.

MATERIALS:

Tablecloth and Napkins

Tablecloth in white (circular or rectangular)
Napkins in white
50cm (20in) red cotton fabric 90cm (36in) wide
Tracing paper
Iron-on interfacing and iron
20cm (8in) square each of white and green cotton, scrap of yellow for candle flames
Stranded embroidery cotton in the following shades:

	DMC	ANCHOR
Red	321	47
Yellow	726	297
Green	702	239
Brown	300	352

Napkin Rings

Cardboard tubing
Scraps of red fabric
Small artificial poinsettia flowers
Fabric glue (spray mount), strong all-purpose glue
Bakable moulding clay in strips 5cm (2in) long and 6mm (¼in) wide (NB you will need one strip per ring)

TABLECLOTH AND NAPKINS

Cut a piece of red fabric slightly larger than flower design, iron a piece of interfacing on to the back. Outline on the tracing paper the pattern pieces of the flowers, leaves and candle; cut out each one and use as a template for transferring shapes onto the relevant coloured fabric pieces, by drawing around each one in soft pencil on the right side of the fabric. The number of flowers etc will depend on the shape and size of your tablecloth. Either a circular or oblong shaped cloth would be suitable for the design.

Begin your motif by placing red fabric with petal outline on the tablecloth in a position of your choice, machine around each petal with small zigzag stitches or hand-stitch with tiny blanket stitches. Repeat for the number of flowers required, then cut the surplus fabric away using sharp embroidery scissors, cutting as close to the stitched edge as possible.

Work the leaves, candles and berries in the same way. Stitch the candle first, then the drips on top of it. Using embroidery cotton, embroider the stems and leaves of the pine sprays in stem stitch (see Techniques). The napkins have an appliquéd berry and embroidered pine spray in one corner.

Tip: If your sewing machine has a scallop edge facility then work all the edges in red to add festive cheer.

NAPKIN RINGS

Cut a ring 5cm (2in) deep out of the cardboard tubing; wrap fabric around the tube, overlapping slightly to gauge the circumference, and allow 10cm (4in) for the depth. Cut out fabric, spray glue onto wrong side; lay the tube ring in the middle of the glued side and wrap fabric around it, overlapping the ends. Tuck the extended fabric inside the ring and press down firmly.

Roll a 5cm (2in) x 6mm (¼in) sausage in the clay, cut the artificial flower heads off their stems and embed one in each end of the clay to make an indentation. Remove the flower and curve the strip to fit the tube, then set the clay in the oven following manufacturer's instructions. Glue the flower heads into the two marked positions on the clay strip and glue to the ring.

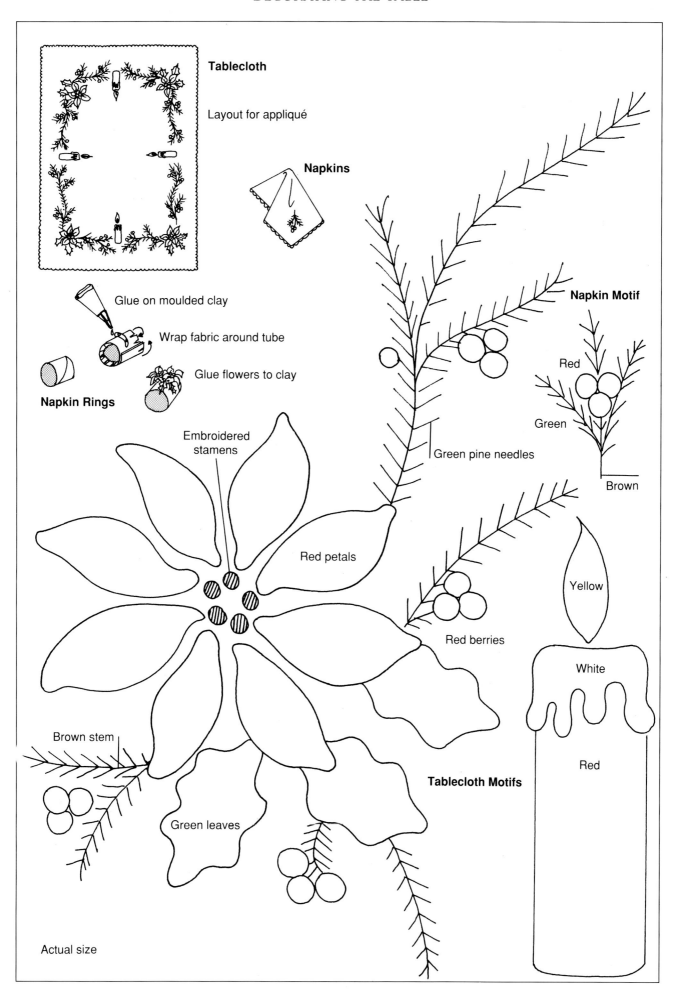

Tablecloth

Layout for appliqué

Napkins

Glue on moulded clay

Wrap fabric around tube

Glue flowers to clay

Napkin Rings

Napkin Motif

Red

Green

Brown

Embroidered stamens

Green pine needles

Red petals

Yellow

Red berries

White

Brown stem

Red

Tablecloth Motifs

Green leaves

Actual size

CHRISTMAS CRACKERS

*C*rackers were first thought of in the 1860s by a sweetmaker called Tom Smith; he used to put small gifts in his sweet wrappers. Over the years these have developed into the sophisticated crackers that we have today. Ours are exceptionally easy to make, and you will have a lot of fun deciding on personal gifts and jokes to fill them.

MATERIALS

A2 59cm x 41cm (23³/₈in x 16¹/₂in) sheet of lightweight paper such as crêpe that will tear easily – one sheet will make approximately three 28cm (11in) long crackers
2 card tube formers (kitchen paper towel rolls are suitable)
String, double-sided sticky tape
Glue
Snaps, mottoes/jokes, gifts, paper hats (from specialist craft shops)
A2 59cm x 41cm (23³/₈in x 16¹/₂in) sheet each of lightweight card and lining paper
Ribbon or decorative cord
String
Trims for decorating: dried flowers, mini cones, herb sachets, artificial flowers, holly, lace, paper doilies, 'Victorian' scraps, ribbons, made frills etc

You can vary the size of crackers by enlarging or reducing the inner card tube support. Make an extra-large one as a special gift, or little ones to decorate the Christmas tree.

Cut a rectangle of crêpe paper 30cm (12in) x 18cm (7in), with grain of crêpe paper following the length, lay flat on work surface; cut a rectangle of lining paper 2.5cm (1in) smaller all around than the crêpe paper. Lay lining paper in the middle of the crêpe paper, put motto and snap on top of it.

Cut a piece of card 14cm (5¹/₂in) x 10cm (4in) and place in the middle on top of the lining paper; the wide part of the card should lie across the length of the lining paper. Cut piece of tube to 10cm (4in) and place in the middle of the paper. At one end of this tube place another to act as a former to make the paper tube. Roll all the layers around the tube, and secure the join with a strip of double-sided sticky tape. Tie a piece of string tightly around the cracker at the point where the formers meet; this will draw up and gather the paper inwards. Carefully slide out the end former, and release the string. Add the gift and paper hat to the cracker through the former that is still in position, then ease this former out.

Insert former up to card on opposite end, tie string around and draw up as for other end, and gently press the former against the card inner tube to give a crisp edge to the outer paper. Slide card tube out, and tie ribbon or decorative cord around the choked ends. Attach chosen trim to the middle of the cracker.

▶ *Christmas Crackers and Red-and-Gold Table Centrepiece*

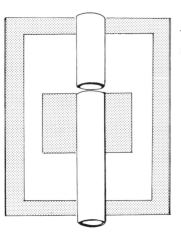

Tube laid on paper ready for wrapping

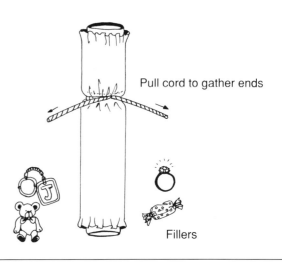

Pull cord to gather ends

Fillers

RED-AND-GOLD TABLE CENTREPIECE

*M*ake *this stunning centrepiece to add the finishing touch to your Christmas table settings.*

MATERIALS

Straw or foam ring, 30cm (12in) diameter
2 bunches of sea lavender (*Statice dumosa*)
Assortment of seed pods, walnuts, cones etc
Artificial gold sprays of mini cones, 6 artificial
gold pears, 6 bunches of artificial gold grapes
6 each of red and gold poinsettia flowers
2 gold bows in florist's crinkle paper
Can of florist's spray in gold
Florist's stub wires, florist's cutters
4 pronged candle-holders, 4 gold candles
Glue

Begin by spraying the lavender, walnuts etc with gold spray. When dry, insert 20cm (8in) lengths of sea lavender around the ring. Fix in position the four candle-holders (these should be on the inner edge of the ring).

To wire the decorations, twist the stub wires or florist wire around the stems on the sprays and on the fruits, securing wire and stem together. Insert the wired sprays and fruits etc around the ring, twisting in the wire stems amongst the straw or dry foam. Finally, wire two crinkle paper bows as for sprays and fix to each side of the ring; insert candles in the holders.

Tip: This would also make an elegant wall garland, by omitting the candles and holders.

Spray candle-holders gold

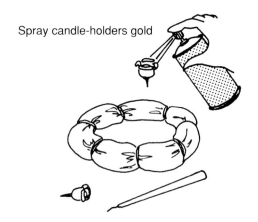

Insert fruit and flowers into ring

SAFETY FIRST *Owing to the straw and dried trims used, the candles must not be lit and left to burn in an unoccupied room.*

STIFFENED CROCHET BASKET

*F**ollowing this simple technique you can make a variety of decorative baskets for sweets, biscuits or flowers.*

MATERIALS

Ready-made crochet mat
Sugar and water solution (method below)
Cardboard
Pins
Clingfilm
String
Former (jamjar)
Ribbon
Crochet hook size 1.25 (UK 3, USA 8) and
cotton Anchor Pelicano No 5 white
(see Techniques for crochet terms)

Make up the sugar solution from one cup of sugar and one cup of hot water fully dissolved over heat. Soak the mat in this and wring out excess liquid.

Place the jamjar upside down on the cardboard, cover it with clingfilm and lay the mat over it. Tie the string around the neck of the jar, choking up the fabric and forming gathers.

Stretch out the points of the mat and pin down on the cardboard. Allow to set overnight; when dry, carefully remove the mat from the jamjar and clingfilm.

Crochet a 35cm (14in) length of chain stitches, and work across them in a 2 trb 2 ch 2 trb 2 ch pattern. Double crochet all around the piece to firm up the edges; this piece forms the handle of the basket. Stiffen as before, mould around the side of a saucepan to form a curve and allow to set before threading ribbon through.

Thread ribbon around the outer edge of the basket, and glue the handle in position on inside of rim.

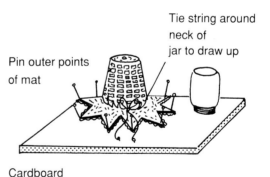

Pin outer points of mat

Tie string around neck of jar to draw up

Cardboard

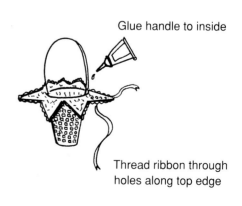

Glue handle to inside

Thread ribbon through holes along top edge

CHAPTER SIX

GIFTS FOR
ADULTS

HIS AND HER WAISTCOATS

A version of the waistcoat has been around since the sixteenth century. Recently it has become a popular unisex item. Make yours in brocade or rich tapestry *fabric with contrast satin back to add a touch of romanticism to your Christmas wardrobe. Made in wool, cotton or denim they would look just as good worn over a pair of jeans.*

MATERIALS

Chest/bust	76-81cm	87-92cm	92-102cm	107-112cm
	30-32in	34-36in	38-40in	42-44in
USA	Petite	Small	Medium	Large
Length	55cm (21½in)	56cm (22¼in)	58cm (22¾in)	59cm (23¼in)
Main fabric 150cm (60in)	70cm (27in)	70cm (27in)	80cm (32in)	80cm (32in)
Lining 115cm (45in)	115cm (45in)	140cm (55in)	140cm (55in)	200cm (80in)

Dressmaker's tracing paper
4 buttons for covering yourself (follow manufacturer's instructions for method)
Scraps of velvet

Tip: If you are using lightweight fabric, interface the front edges with iron-on interfacing to help support the buttons and buttonholes.

Grade up the patterns to size (see Techniques) and make a note of all markings onto the tracing paper. Make any length alterations necessary at this point. Using cutting layout instructions, cut two fronts and pockets in main fabric; four backs, two fronts and two belt strips in lining fabric. If you want the outer part of your waistcoat all in the same fabric cut two backs and two belt pieces in main fabric. Take care, when cutting out fabric with a patterned design, that the fronts and welt pockets match up.

With right sides together fold pocket welt in half along width of fabric, press folded edge and machine 12mm (½in) seam at both sides; trim machined seam. Turn right way out and push corners out with a blunt point such as a knitting needle; press edges. Repeat for other welt piece.

Place the pocket on the front of the waistcoat at marked points. The raw edge of the finished pocket should be at the top and the folded edge facing down with right sides together. Machine across the raw edges on both pockets, trim seam and press upwards. Stitch the sides of the pocket to the main body fabric.

With right sides together, machine centre back seams first on inner and then on outer back pieces. Trim seams and press open; with right sides together pin the main fabric front pieces to the outer back lining piece at the shoulders, and machine shoulder seams. Repeat for front and back lining pieces, trim and press all seams open.

Fold belt pieces in half on the long edge of fabric, right sides together; machine one short and one long edge of each belt. Trim the seam, turn to the right side (pushing out corners) and press flat. Pin belt pieces on the right side of the back piece at side seam edge where marked, and stitch in position.

With right sides together pin the front and back pieces together with the side seams open. Machine around outer edges at front, neck, armholes and lower edges. Trim seams and snip up to seam edge where curved. Turn to the right side by passing the fronts through the shoulders and out at the sides. Press all outer edges, then top stitch 6mm (¼in) in all round. Pin edges of side seams together on the inside of the fabric, machine seams enclosing belt and continue stitching 2.5cm (1in) upwards and downwards onto lining section. Trim seams and press open.

On the right side of front lining piece at the sideseam, press a 1cm (½in) folded edge over to the wrong side, lay the edge of the back lining piece under the front and close up the lining opening with small stitches. Make four buttonholes corresponding to 'his' or 'her' fastenings. Cover buttons with velvet and sew on as marked. Tie the belt in a knot at the centre back.

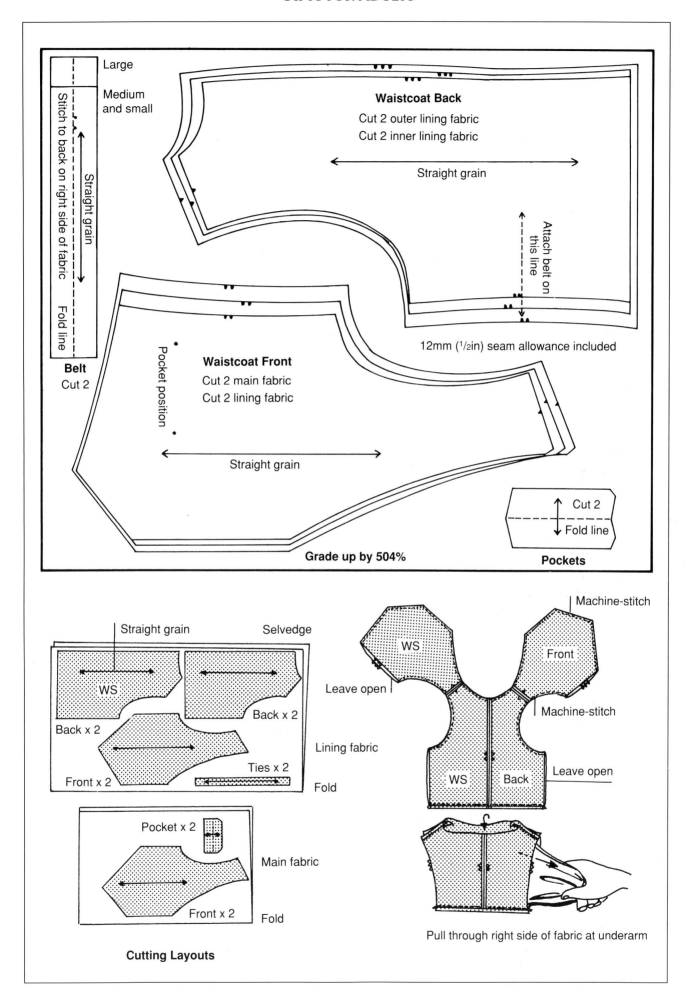

Belt
Cut 2

Large

Medium and small

Stitch to back on right side of fabric

Straight grain

Fold line

Waistcoat Back
Cut 2 outer lining fabric
Cut 2 inner lining fabric

Straight grain

Attach belt on this line

12mm (½in) seam allowance included

Pocket position

Waistcoat Front
Cut 2 main fabric
Cut 2 lining fabric

Straight grain

Cut 2
Fold line

Grade up by 504%

Pockets

Straight grain   Selvedge

WS

Back x 2

Back x 2

Front x 2

Ties x 2

Lining fabric

Fold

Pocket x 2

Front x 2

Main fabric

Fold

Cutting Layouts

Machine-stitch

WS

Front

Leave open

Machine-stitch

WS   Back

Leave open

Pull through right side of fabric at underarm

HIS AND HER BOUDOIR SLIPPERS

*I*f *you plan to spend Christmas away, then make these lightweight slippers to take with you; or make some for your guests as a welcoming present. In stretch towelling they are ideal to wear in the bathroom.*

MATERIALS

Fabric 40cm x 90cm (16in x 36in)
Heavyweight interfacing 40cm x 90cm
(16in x 36in)
3m (120in) bias binding 2.5cm (1in) wide
Rubber-backed heat resistant table cover fabric
40cm x 90cm (16in x 36in), or 2 cork soles
15cm (6in) polyester wadding 45cm (18in) wide
for quilting
Card
Strong fabric glue
Bought trim ideas: ribbon rose, ribbon bow, initials
or iron-on motif.

Trace around your foot and outline curves as the pattern overleaf.

Trace sole and upper onto card, cut out and use as a template. For one slipper cut a sole out of interfacing, fabric and rubber-backed fabric. Cut two uppers out of fabric, and one upper out of wadding. Repeat for the other foot, but reverse the template. Sandwich one piece of wadding between two of the upper pieces, making sure fabric is right side out on top and bottom. Cut a length of binding to fit the inner edge of the upper piece, fold it in half over raw edge. Tack all layers and then machine in position close to unfolded edge. Repeat for the other upper piece.

Tack a sole fabric piece onto the sole interfacing piece, ensuring the right side of the fabric is uppermost.

Lay underside of upper to fit on top side of the sole piece, and tack through all thicknesses. Cut a length of binding long enough to fit around the sole, allowing a bit to tuck in for neatening. Starting on the inside edge of sole, pin folded binding over the edge of the sole, incorporating the upper sections and tucking in ends of binding. Tack in position and then machine close to outer edge of binding, easing it around the curves.

Remove all tacking threads, press with a damp cloth and iron. Glue the interfacing side of the sole onto the rubber sole. Finish off with chosen trim.

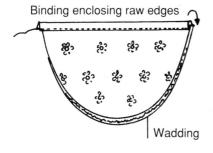

Binding enclosing raw edges

Wadding

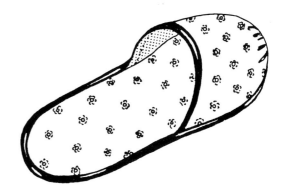

Bind all the way around sole, incorporating upper

◄ *His and Her Waistcoats*

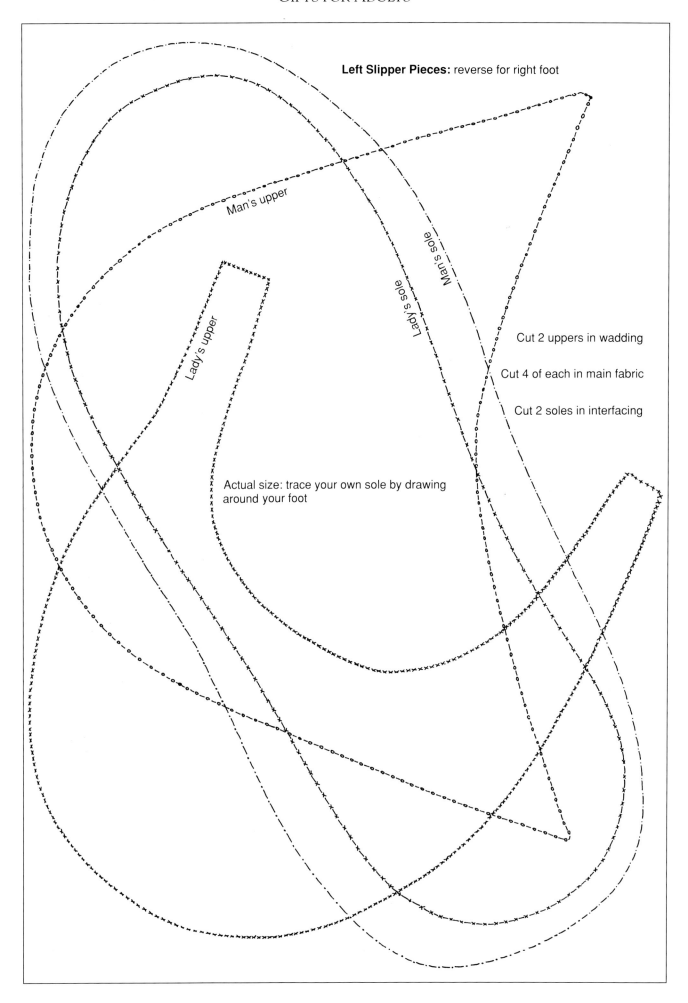

Left Slipper Pieces: reverse for right foot

Man's upper

Man's sole

Lady's sole

Lady's upper

Cut 2 uppers in wadding

Cut 4 of each in main fabric

Cut 2 soles in interfacing

Actual size: trace your own sole by drawing around your foot

TRIMMED FACE MIT, FLANNEL AND TOWEL

*T*hese are always useful to have and easy to make. If you have visitors staying over Christmas make them their own versions as an extra-special gift.

MATERIALS

30cm (12in) towelling fabric 90cm (36in) wide
1m (40in) printed ribbon 2.5cm (1in) wide for
flannel and towel, and 50cm (20in) x 3.5cm
(1¹/2in) wide for mit
Tracing paper
Bought flannel and towel
Heart shape soap, tree soap
Approx 10cm (4in) ribbon 6mm (¹/4in) wide
for loops
Glue

Trace around your hand onto some paper, turn shape into an oblong to fit around your hand with 6mm (¹/4in) seam allowance, and cut out two in towelling. Use the selvedge of the fabric for the top edge of the mit to save hemming.

Lay a strip of ribbon across each oblong 3cm (1¹/4in) from the top and machine on all the way around, tucking the ribbon under at the ends. Zigzag stitch the outer raw edges to neaten, lay ribbon-trimmed sides on top of each other and machine around 6mm (¹/4in) in from outer edge. Turn to the right side, sew on a ribbon hanging loop. Trim the towel and flannel with ribbon sewn on in the same fashion as above.

Make a small bow and sew onto the middle of the towel ribbon.

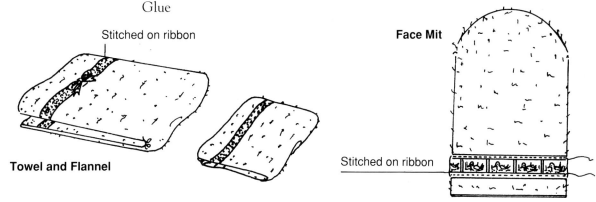

Stitched on ribbon

Towel and Flannel

Face Mit

Stitched on ribbon

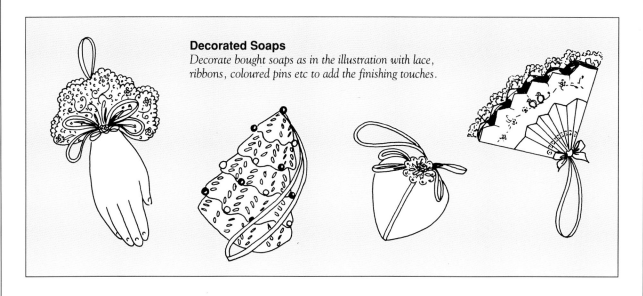

Decorated Soaps
Decorate bought soaps as in the illustration with lace, ribbons, coloured pins etc to add the finishing touches.

BOXER SHORTS

*M*ake these fun boxer shorts for the man in your life in a discreet Christmas print, or in silk for added luxury. As they have a closed fly opening they would look good in a lovely print to wear on the beach.

MATERIALS

1.2m (48in) fabric 90cm (36in) wide
1.2m (48in) elastic 12mm (^{1}/2in) wide
3 buttons approximately 12mm (^{1}/2in) in diameter
Dressmaker's paper
Small safety pin for threading elastic

Sizes	Small
Waist	71-76cm (28-30in)
Hips	89-94cm (35-37in)

Medium	Large
81-87cm (32-34in)	92-99cm (36-39in)
99-104cm (39-41in)	109-114cm (43-45in)

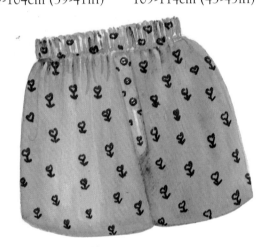

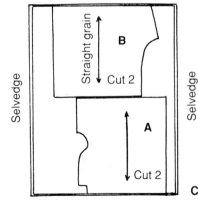

Cutting layout

Grade up pattern (see Techniques) onto dressmaker's paper. Lengthen or shorten pattern pieces at this stage. Following indicated cutting directions, cut out two front and two back pieces. Neaten all raw edges except sides and waist with zigzag machine stitch. Stitch front piece A to back piece B at inner leg matching points, using 12mm (^{1}/2in) seam allowance. Press seam open, repeat for other two front and back pieces.

Pin centre back and front pieces together with right sides facing each other; begin machining for 6mm (^{1}/4in); leave open for 2cm (^{3}/4in) for elastic insert, then continue stitching all the way around the crotch seam up to large dot marked on pattern. Leave open between large dots and complete stitching to top of the waist. Strengthen the crotch by a double row of machining at the curved edge. Clip up to seam line at curves and into large dots below opening and on the right seam section above opening. This will allow the fly extension to lie flat on the left inside section. Press crotch seam on inside, turn to the right side and press fly opening. Top stitch through all the layers of fabric around the fly curve marked on the pattern.

French seam the side seams (see Techniques).

Elastic casing: press 6mm (^{1}/4in) under on the inside top edge, fold band in half and tack in position. Machine three rows of stitching around the waistband, one at the top edge, one in the middle and one at the bottom, to make channels to encase elastic. Cut two pieces of elastic each 2.5cm (1in) more than waist measurement, attach two safety pins at one end of each length of elastic and thread through the channels. Secure other end of elastic to pins and try on for size; adjust to fit. Join ends of elastic with small stitches, then close opening with slip stitches.

Make a narrow hem by pressing up 6mm (^{1}/4in) around each lower edge of leg, and turning under 2cm (^{3}/4in). Press. Machine close to top and lower edges of hem. Stitch buttons to left side of fly opening. Press to finish off.

BOXER SHORTS

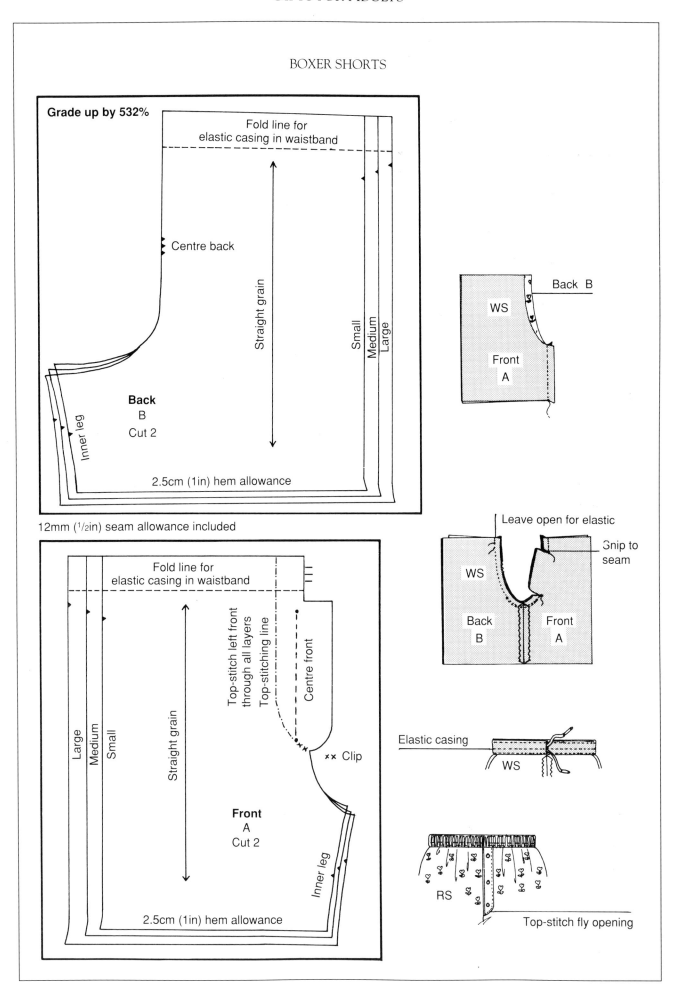

Grade up by 532%

Fold line for
elastic casing in waistband

Centre back

Straight grain

Small
Medium
Large

Back
B
Cut 2

Inner leg

2.5cm (1in) hem allowance

12mm (½in) seam allowance included

Back B

WS

Front
A

Fold line for
elastic casing in waistband

Large
Medium
Small

Straight grain

Top-stitch left front through all layers
Top-stitching line
Centre front

Front
A
Cut 2

Inner leg

xx Clip

2.5cm (1in) hem allowance

Leave open for elastic

Snip to seam

WS

Back
B

Front
A

Elastic casing

WS

RS

Top-stitch fly opening

HOT WATER BOTTLE COVER

Long gone are the days when the maid warmed the beds with a pan of red hot coals; electric blankets and central heating have seen an end to that practice. However, nothing can match the cosiness of a hot water bottle. This pretty cover will protect you from burning.

MATERIALS:

45cm (18in) cotton fabric 115cm (45in) wide
45cm (18in) x 115cm (45in) piece of polyester
wadding 12mm (^{1}/2in) thick
1.5m (60in) bias binding 2.5cm (1in) wide
2 press-studs
Tracing paper and card
35cm (14in) ribbon 2.5cm (1in) wide

Trace around a bought hot water bottle, shaping as illustrated; add 6mm (^{1}/4in) seam allowance. Fold fabric in half and sandwich the wadding within it; tack around the edge. Start quilting from the centre of the fabric by machining outwards to the sides, stitching in vertical lines 2.5cm (1in) apart. Using template, cut out two bottle shapes in the quilted fabric.

Fold a 40cm (15^1/2in) length of binding in half; pin this around the top of one bottle section, enclosing the raw edges; tack and then machine close to outer unfolded edge, right side uppermost. Lay other bottle shape on top of bound one. Starting in the middle of the bottom edge, pin some folded binding around the shape, enclosing all thicknesses and working from left to right. Turn in end over join, tack and machine on binding as before, taking care where fabric is several layers thick. Iron, and sew on bow, and press-studs in marked positions.

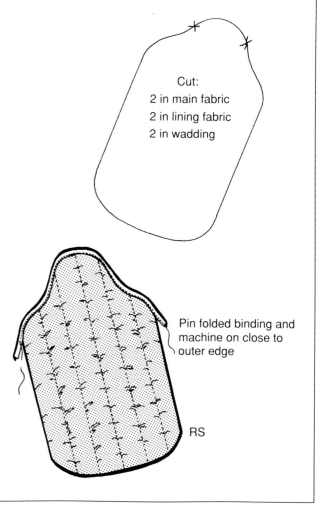

Cut:
2 in main fabric
2 in lining fabric
2 in wadding

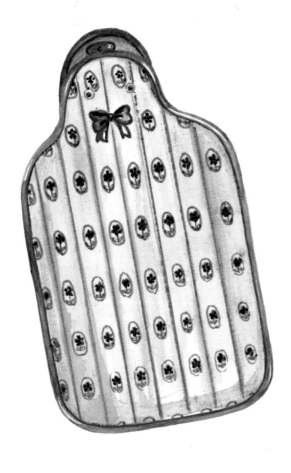

Pin folded binding and machine on close to outer edge

RS

APRON BOTTLE COVERS

*M*ake plain versions of these covers and write the name of a member of your family on each one; dress the bottles of beer or juice and stand them at the side of each place setting.

MATERIALS

Scraps of plain and printed cotton fabrics, felt
Bias binding
Iron-on interfacing
Card
Tracing paper
Fabric marker pens
Holly or ribbon rose trims
2 small white buttons

Grade up and trace shape of apron onto card, and cut out in fabric and interfacing. Bond the interfacing to the back of the fabric with an iron. Neaten the top edge of the apron by turning 6mm (¼in) under on the wrong side and machining across lower edge.

Cut a 29.5cm (11½in) length of binding, fold in half and pin to enclose the lower curved edge; machine in place, going up the left side and down the right side. Cut another length of binding 74cm (29in), allowing a 23cm (9in) extension for the left tie. Pin folded binding to left edge of apron, enclosing raw edge of fabric. Allow 12cm (5in) for a neck loop at the top and pin binding down right side, with a 23cm (9in) extension free for the right tie. Machine all the way round, beginning from the left side and ending at the end of the right tie.

On the plain version write names or make a design in fabric marker pens and press with hot iron to seal the ink and make the apron washable.

Method for dinner jacket is similar, but cut a V out of the felt at the neck point and stitch a piece of white fabric on the underside to simulate a shirt; glue on buttons, rose and bow tie.

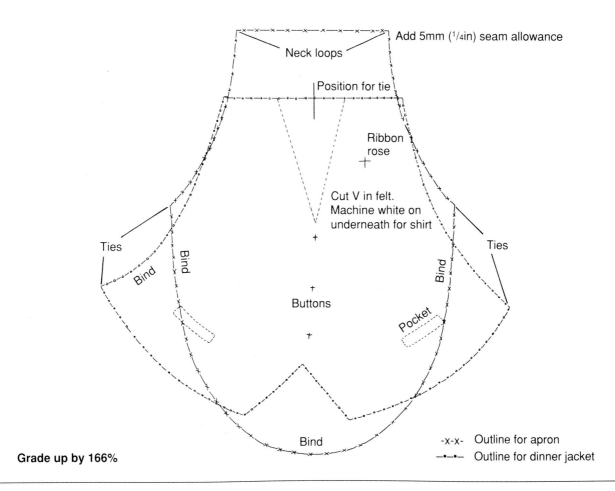

Add 5mm (¼in) seam allowance
Neck loops
Position for tie
Ribbon rose
Cut V in felt. Machine white on underneath for shirt
Ties
Bind
Bind
Ties
Buttons
Bind
Pocket
Bind

-x-x- Outline for apron
—•—•— Outline for dinner jacket

Grade up by 166%

HER HALF-APRON AND OVEN GLOVES

Make this attractive set to protect your Christmas outfit. You will look very smart if you serve at the table and forget to take it off!

MATERIALS

Apron

1m (40in) print fabric 115cm (45in) wide

3m (120in) gathered broderie anglaise 6cm (2^1/2in) wide

3m (120in) satin ribbon 6mm (^{1}/4in) wide

61cm (24in) strip of iron-on interfacing 4cm (1^1/2in) wide

Oven Gloves

50cm (20in) fabric 115cm (45in) wide

25cm (10in) wadding for quilting, 115cm (45in) wide

2.5m (100in) bias binding 2.5cm (1in) wide

APRON

Cut apron piece of fabric 58.5cm (23in) long using the full width of fabric; and pocket piece 19cm (7^1/2in) x 17cm (6^1/2in). Turn under 12mm (^{1}/2in) hem at the sides and the base of the fabric; machine close to the outer edge. Run two rows of gathering stitches across the top edge and draw up.

Cut three strips of fabric 61cm (24in) long x 7.5cm (3in) wide. Fold two of them (for apron ties) in half lengthways, right sides together, and machine stitch, taking a 6mm (^{1}/4in) seam allowance, along long edge and one short edge. Turn to the right side and push out ends with a blunt point; press seam. Use the third strip for the waistband; fold it in half lengthwise with wrong sides together and press the folded edge. Cut a strip of interfacing to fit along half of the folded piece and iron in position. Fold up a 6mm (^{1}/4in) turning along the edge of strip and press. Place the right side of the gathered edge of the apron under the folded edge of the waistband and machine all layers together on the right side 6mm (^{1}/4in) in from edge. Fold over and hand-stitch the raw edge on the inside of the waist band covering the seam. Insert the apron ties at each end of the open waistband, turning under 6mm (^{1}/4in) hem; machine through all layers securing the ends.

Thread the ribbon through the broderie anglaise channel. Pin the broderie around the outer edges of the apron and machine close to outer edge. Turn in a 12mm (^{1}/2in) hem on the top edge of the pocket piece and machine on the wrong side. Pin and sew broderie onto the edge of the right side of the pocket, then place pocket right side up on the left-hand side of apron facing you, 15.5cm (6in) from top of waistband and 10cm (4in) in from the side edge. Machine all around on the outer edge of the broderie channel. Make a small bow and sew in the middle of lower edge of the pocket.

OVEN GLOVES

Cut two strips across the fabric 70cm (27^1/2in) wide x 20cm (7^3/4in) deep, and four pocket pieces 18.5cm (7^1/4in) wide x 20cm (7^3/4in) deep. Cut three pieces of wadding to match fabric outer sections. Sandwich together: to make a sandwich of the wadding, take one fabric piece and lay flat with right side down, onto this lay the wadding and then on top another matching fabric piece with right side uppermost. Curve all corners on the strips and one end of pocket pieces. Quilt the pieces together vertically down the length of the fabric, stitching rows 5cm (2in) apart.

Pin length of folded binding over the straight edge of each pocket piece, enclosing raw edges, and machine close to unfolded edge. Lay a pocket at each end of the quilted strip, matching curved edges. Pin folded binding at the centre all the way around the strip, enclosing all raw edges and all pocket layers. Machine close to unfolded edge, and turn in bias binding where ends meet. Press the oven gloves.

HER HALF APRON AND OVEN GLOVES

▲ *Apron, Oven Mit and Chef's Hat; Half-Apron and Oven Gloves*

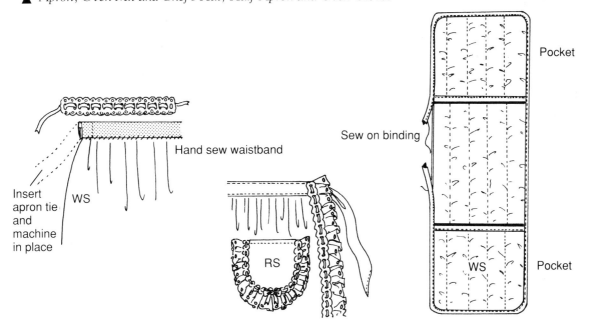

Hand sew waistband

Insert apron tie and machine in place

WS

Sew on binding

Pocket

RS

WS

Pocket

HIS APRON, OVEN MIT AND CHEF'S HAT

Christmas lunch is always a busy time in the kitchen. Be well prepared and make the man in your life a suit of armour so he can join in with the chores!

MATERIALS

Apron

1m (40in) cotton ticking 90cm (36in) wide
2.5m (100in) bias binding 12mm (^{1}/$_2$in) wide
56cm (22in) woven tape 4cm (1^1/$_2$in) wide
1.4m (55in) woven tape 2.5cm (1in) wide
Tracing paper

Oven Mit

2 pieces of ticking, 30cm (12in) x 25cm (10in)
2 pieces of cotton lining, 30cm (12in) x 25cm (10in)
1m (40in) bias binding 2.5cm (1in) wide
2 pieces of wadding for quilting, 30cm (12in) x 25cm (10in)

Chef's Hat

60cm (24in) cotton ticking 90cm (36in) wide
6cm (2^1/$_2$in) elastic 6mm (^{1}/$_4$in) wide

APRON

Grade up the pattern onto tracing paper (see Techniques); cut one apron out in fabric, following cutting instructions. Turn under a 12mm (^{1}/$_2$in) hem on the top edge of the apron and machine close to the edge. Hem sides and the bottom edge with a 2.5cm (1in) hem. Press all edges. Machine bias binding on, enclosing the two curved edges; turn in the ends of binding to neaten.

Using 56cm (22in) length of the 4cm (1^1/$_2$in) wide tape sew onto the outer edges of the top of the apron for the neck loop. For ties, cut two 70cm (27^1/$_2$in) lengths of the 2.5cm (1in) wide tape and machine to the top of each side edge. Neaten free ends with a small hand-stitched hem.

Cut pocket shape on vertical grain of fabric. Turning under 6mm (^{1}/$_4$in), pin the pocket to the centre front and machine on the right side close to folded edge. Machine vertically down the middle of the pocket to divide in two.

OVEN MIT

Take one piece of ticking and one of lining, and sandwich one piece of wadding in between. Quilt by machine, following the vertical lines and spacing 4cm (1^1/$_2$in) apart for each row. Repeat with remaining pieces. Grade up the outline and cut a mit shape out of each quilted piece.

With lining sides of mit together, cut a length of bias binding long enough to bind outer curved edges of the mit, and pin around enclosing raw edges. Machine close to the outer edge of the binding. Cut a length of binding to neaten the top edge of the mit, and machine as before, catching in on the left side a hanging loop made from some binding.

CHEF'S HAT

Cut a circle of fabric 38cm (15in) diameter for the crown, and a strip 60cm (23^1/$_2$in) x 15.5cm (6in) for the hat band.

Machine the short edges of the strip together on wrong side, then fold joined-up strip in half lengthwise, and press. On the inside folded edge, machine length of elastic to the seam 8cm (3in) out from the seam: this will draw the head circumference in to fit different head sizes. Run two rows of gathering stitches along outer edge of the crown circle and draw up to fit the hat band. Pin the band and the circular piece right sides together, machine on the wrong side taking 12mm (^{1}/$_2$in) seam allowance. Hem by hand inner edge of the band to cover the seam.

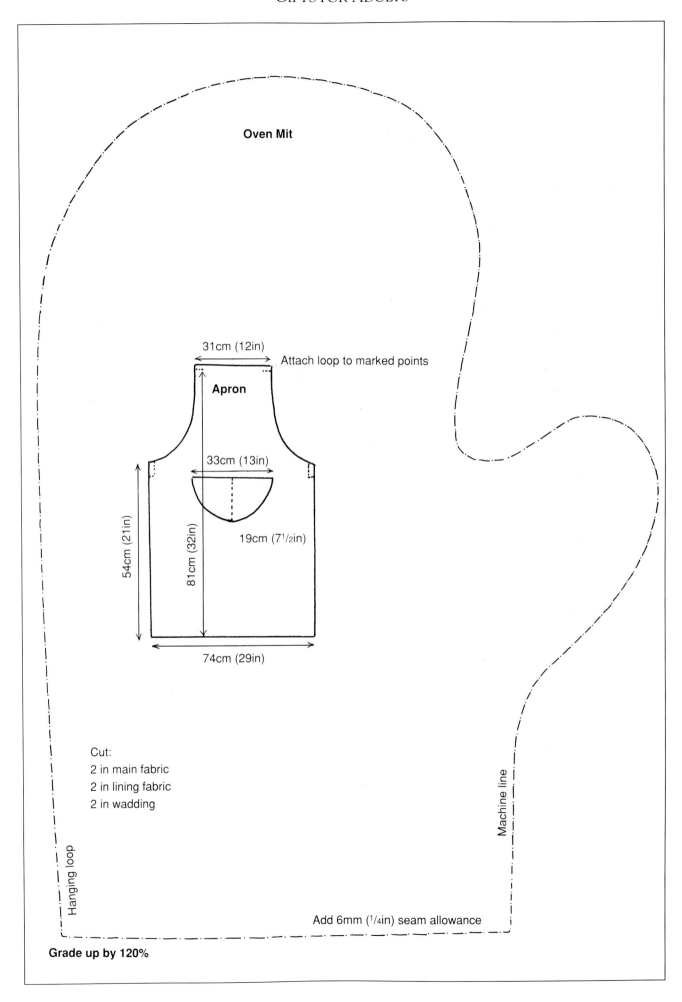

Oven Mit

31cm (12in)

Attach loop to marked points

Apron

33cm (13in)

19cm (7¹/₂in)

54cm (21in)

81cm (32in)

74cm (29in)

Cut:
2 in main fabric
2 in lining fabric
2 in wadding

Hanging loop

Machine line

Add 6mm (¹/₄in) seam allowance

Grade up by 120%

FABRIC-COVERED ALBUM AND DIARY

*O*nce you have mastered the principles of this technique, you will find all kinds of uses for it. Recipe books, visitor's books and many more.

MATERIALS

Bought album/diary
Cotton fabric
Spray-on fabric glue, all-purpose glue
Oval card picture mount
Piping cord, broderie anglaise
Lining paper
One button you can cover yourself (see manufacturer's instructions for method) and velvet scrap
Cord tassel, velvet ribbon

Cut the fabric 2.5cm (1in) wider than the album all around. Spray glue onto the wrong side of the fabric and lay the album, opened out, on top of this side of the fabric. Stretch the fabric over the covers and press down, pushing out any air bubbles and creases.

Mitre all the corners and snip up to edge of the album the width of the spine; tuck in this flap at the top and bottom. Fold over to the inside the top and bottom overlapping pieces, and both side pieces. Define the edges and the spine of the album with your thumbnail.

Cut two pieces of lining paper to fit flush with the inside of the album covers and glue in place concealing the turnings.

Glue the right side of the picture mount to the wrong side of the fabric. Make a hole in the middle of this and snip up to the inner edge of the oval mount. Tuck the overlapping flaps over the edge to the back and glue down. Glue some piping cord around the outer edge of the picture mount; gather up broderie anglaise to form a circle and glue at the back of the piped edge. Right side of broderie should be facing upwards to the right side of the picture mount. Glue the mount to the front of the album on side and bottom edges to enable a photograph to be inserted from the top. Make a rosette of broderie by gathering up a 25cm (10in) length with small running stitches and drawing up tightly. Cover a button with some velvet and stitch to the middle of the rosette, glue in position on the front of album.

For the diary follow the method up to covering the picture mount. Insert and knot a cord tassel through the spine of the album, or glue a velvet ribbon marker in the top edge of the diary.

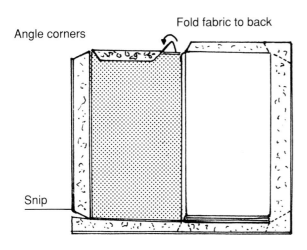

Angle corners

Fold fabric to back

Snip

Snip fabric and tuck into spine

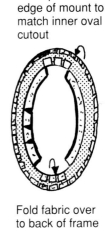

Cut square outer edge of mount to match inner oval cutout

Fold fabric over to back of frame

HIGHLAND SCOTTIE HAT AND SCARF SET

Make this charming hat and scarf set teamed up with its matching brooch as a gift for a friend or relative. Something they will welcome for the coming chilly winter days.

MATERIALS

Pair 3¹/4mm (UK 10, USA 3) knitting needles
Pair 4mm (UK 8, USA 6) knitting needles

Hat

(Fits average lady's head)
50g (2oz) ball of red double knit wool
25g (1oz) ball of black double knit wool
38cm (15in) ribbon 2mm (¹/8in) wide

Scarf

5 x 50g (2oz) balls of red double knit wool
25g (1oz) ball of black knitting wool
Scissors and card

Tension: on 4mm (UK 8, USA 6), 23 sts and 30 rows in st st = 10cm (4in)
(For knitting terms and methods, see Techniques)

HAT

Cast on 116 sts on 3¹/4mm (UK 10, USA 3) size needles in the red and work in K1, P1, rib for 3cm (1¹/4in), increasing on last row by 5 sts evenly across the row (121 sts). Change to 4mm (UK 8, USA 6) needles and, beginning with a knit row, work following four rows in stocking stich (K1 row, P1 row sequence). Work the next 15 rows from the chart, joining in the black as required, and repeating the motif nine times across the work. At the end of the 15th row break off the black yarn and continue in the red. Work a further 3 rows in stocking stitch.

Crown shaping: First row: * knit 13 sts, K2tog: repeat from * to last stitch, K1. Second and every

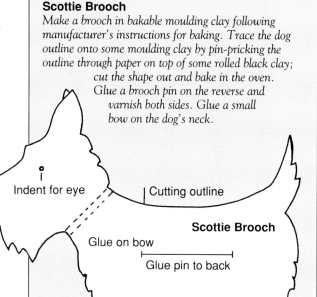

Scottie Brooch
Make a brooch in bakable moulding clay following manufacturer's instructions for baking. Trace the dog outline onto some moulding clay by pin-pricking the outline through paper on top of some rolled black clay; cut the shape out and bake in the oven. Glue a brooch pin on the reverse and varnish both sides. Glue a small bow on the dog's neck.

Indent for eye | Cutting outline

Scottie Brooch

Glue on bow
Glue pin to back

Actual size

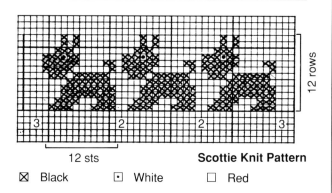

12 rows

3   2   2   3

12 sts   **Scottie Knit Pattern**

☒ Black   ⊡ White   ☐ Red

alternate row purl. Third row: * K12, K2tog; repeat from * to last stitch, K1. Fifth row: * K11, K2tog; repeat from * to last stitch, K1. Seventh row: * K10 sts, K2tog: repeat from * to last stitch K1. Continue decreasing in this way until 33 sts remain. Following row: P1, * P2tog, P2; repeat from * to end of the row. Next row: * K1, K2tog; repeat to the end. Next row P1, * P2tog; repeat from * to end of row (total 9 sts). Break off yarn, and thread end back through the stitches, draw up and knot together. Press on wrong side with iron

and damp cloth, back-stitch seam together. Turn right side out, make a bow in the ribbon and sew onto dog's neck, on the left side of hat as worn.

SCARF

In red yarn, cast on 121 sts using 4mm (UK 8, USA 6) needles. Work 10cm (4in) in stocking stitch ending with a purl row. Work the fifteen rows from the chart joining in black yarn as required. The pattern is repeated across the scarf nine times. Break off the black and continue in stocking stitch for 152cm (60in). Join in the black and work fifteen pattern rows from chart in reverse order, break off black and continue in stocking stitch for 10cm (4in). Cast off, and break yarn. Press long edges with iron and damp cloth, back-stitch to close up seam and hems.

Make a fringe by wrapping wool ten times around two pieces of card 20cm (8in) long. Cut through the looped ends and insert in the hem of the scarf tying in a knot. (See Techniques for diagram.) Repeat across the edge at evenly spaced intervals. Trim ends of fringe.

KNITTED HAT AND SCARF SET WITH FIR TREE MOTIF

Make this snug hat and scarf set for your favourite man: it is sure to be well received with chills of winter in the air.

MATERIALS

Hat

(Hat fits average man's head)
Two 50g (2oz) balls double knit yarn in navy
25g (1oz) ball double knit yarn in emerald
Pair of 3¹/4mm (UK 10) (USA 3) knitting-needles
Pair of 4mm (UK8) (USA 6) knitting-needles
Scissors and card

Scarf

Six 50g (2oz) balls double knitting yarn in navy
25g (1oz) ball double knitting yarn in emerald
Pair of 4mm (UK 8, USA 6) knitting needles
Scissors and card
Tension: on 4mm (UK 8, USA 6), 22 sts and 30 rows in st st = 10cm (4in).
(For knitting terms and methods, see Techniques)

HAT

Cast on 127 sts in navy using 3¹/4mm (UK 10, USA 3) needles, work the first row in rib on the right side K1, * P1, K1, repeat from * to the end of the row. Next row P1, * K1, P1; repeat from * to the end of the row. Continue in this sequence for 14cm (5¹/2in) ending on a second row. Change to 4mm (UK 8, USA 6) needles and, beginning with a knit row, continue in stocking stitch (K1 row, P1 row); follow the pattern from the chart and join in the emerald as required working pattern nine times across the work. When chart is complete break off green yarn and continue in stocking stitch until hat measures 26cm (10in), ending on a purl row.

Shape the crown by knitting 13 sts, K2tog, K10, K2tog; eight times, K13, K2tog, K1 (total 117 sts). Following row purl to end. Next row K12, K2tog, K9, K2tog, eight times; K12, K2tog, K1 (total, 107 sts). Following row purl. Continue decreasing in the same way until 27 sts remain ending on a purl row. Next row K3tog three times, K2tog four times, K3tog three times, K1 (total 11 sts). Break off yarn and draw up end through the remaining stitches and knot. Press the edges with a damp cloth and iron, backstitch the seam together on the reverse side. Make a pompon by cutting two circles in card 5cm (2in) in diameter with the middles cut out, placing them together, and wrapping wool through until the hole is closed up; slit wool at outer edge and tie a length of wool between the two layers of card, drawing up the wool to a ball; tie a knot. Secure to the top of the hat with firm stitches. (See Techniques for diagram.) Turn up the brim of the hat to the outside.

SCARF

Cast on 127 sts on 4mm (UK 8, USA 6) needles in navy. Work 14cm (5¹/2in) in stocking stitch, then follow the pattern rows from the chart, joining in and breaking off the green as required. Continue in stocking stich for 152cm (60in). Join in the green and work the pattern from the chart in the reverse order, then break off green yarn. Continue in st st for 14 cm (5¹/2in) then cast off. Press the edges with iron and a damp cloth and backstitch together, closing up the sides and hems. Press the seam to the centre on the back. Make tassels using same method as scarf on page 105.

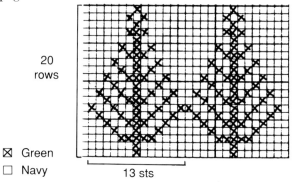

20 rows

13 sts

☒ Green
☐ Navy

LADY'S EVENING POCHETTE

Make this delightful bag in a sophisticated print, or if you are feeling adventurous then fashion it in quilted velvet.

MATERIALS

35cm (14in) fabric 90cm (36in) wide
Polyester wadding
1m (40in) satin bias binding 2.5cm (1in) wide
Press-stud 6mm ($\frac{1}{4}$in) diameter, button, tassel
Tracing paper
1m (40in) satin cord, 12mm ($\frac{1}{2}$in) diameter

Trace the outline of the bag and cut out two whole pieces and two half pieces in fabric and one each in wadding. Sandwich the wadding between the fabric sections. Fold a strip of binding over the top straight edge of the half piece to conceal raw edges, pin and machine close to inner unfolded edge. Lay the half piece on top of the oval piece and pin a length of folded binding over the raw edges. Machine all the way around through all thicknesses, close to the unfolded edge. Fold the flap of the bag down and press; sew the ends of the cord to each inner side seam.

To complete, sew the press-stud on underside of the flap and in the middle of the front under section. Sew button and tassel to front of the flap at the centre.

Cut
2 x $\frac{1}{2}$ section for front
2 x $\frac{1}{2}$ section on fold for full piece
1 of each in wadding

Extend completely for full oval (back plus flap-over section)

Button position

Cutting and binding edge

Actual size

EASY JEWELLERY

*O*nce you have mastered the basics of making jewellery there is a wealth of ideas open to you. You'll be able to make pieces to match your outfits, pretty pastels for the spring and bright colours for the summer. Use our glamorous ideas to complement your Christmas outfit.

Modelled Victorian Hand and Posy Brooch

Make this traditional Victorian hand and posy brooch in bakable moulding clay, following the manufacturer's instructions for setting. Copy details from the illustration. Spray with bronze paint when cool, and glue on brooch pin at the back to complete.

MATERIALS

Heart Necklace

40 black facet beads, 10mm (^{4}/$_{10}$in) size
70cm (27in) length of nylon line for jewellery
10 small gilt rosebud beads
6 gilt antique disc beads
2 small gilt hogan beads
1 antique gilt heart with loop
(Finished length of necklace: approximately 40cm (16in))
Glue
Sewing needle

Drop Earrings

2 x 10cm (4in) lengths of nylon line for jewellery
2 metal clip triangles
2 ear hooks with loops
2 jet drops
2 lozenge shape jet beads
2 disc shape jet beads

Hat Pin

1 hat pin with attached pearl drop bead
2 black facet beads, 10mm (^{4}/$_{10}$in) size
Crimp tool

NECKLACE

Tie one end of the nylon around the loop on one end of the clasp and secure with a double knot. Allow a 5cm (2in) tail of nylon to thread back through the beads.

Thread the beads in the following sequence: seventeen facet beads, then rose, oval, facet, rose, oval, facet, rose, oval, facet, rose, small hogan, rose. Add the heart, then repeat sequence in reverse for the other side.

Thread tail end of the nylon through the loop to the other end of the clasp and knot twice. Insert both tails of nylon back through the beads. For extra security, dab a small drop of glue on the end of the thread.

EARRINGS

Fit the clip triangle to the drop bead and pinch to close up. Thread the nylon through the ear loop, the lozenge, the disc bead, the clasp and back through the beads, ending with a double knot. Snip off ends of nylon and dab with glue. Repeat for second earring.

HAT PIN

Thread the two black facet beads onto the stem of the pin up to the fixed drop pearl, and crimp below the last bead to secure.

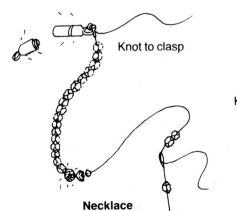

Knot to clasp

Necklace

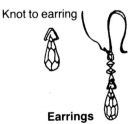

Knot to earring

Earrings

Crimp to secure beads

Hat Pin

CHAPTER SEVEN

GIFTS FOR
CHILDREN

HOBBY HORSE

This charming toy will keep young children occupied for hours, as they go on imaginary rides to Banbury Cross. With some odds and ends it is simple to make.

MATERIALS

50cm (20in) jumbo cord fabric in brown, 90cm (36in) wide
25cm (10in) square of fawn felt, scrap of peach-colour felt
1 pair of toy eyes
1 mop head
2 brass knobs with screw ends to fit cross bar
Polyester wadding
2.5cm (1in) diameter wood dowelling (for long bar)
2cm (3/4in) diameter wood dowelling (for cross bar)
Varnish, mahogany stain and paintbrush
50cm (20in) length of string
1m (40in) braid trim, 1m (40in) fringed braid
30cm (12in) cotton tape 6mm (1/4in) wide
2 brass curtain rings, 10 brass bells

Grade up the pattern pieces onto paper (see Techniques) and cut out two head and ear sections in cord fabric, and two ear fronts in fawn felt. Machine the felt and cord ear pieces together on the wrong side of the fabric; as the felt ear is smaller it will draw the cord around to the front when turned to the right side. Trim raw edges, snip curves and turn to the right side, press machined edges.

Machine the head pieces together on the wrong side leaving open at marked points. Snip up to seamline on curved edges, turn to the right side and press the seam flat using the point of the iron.

Cut two circles of the peach felt 6mm (1/4in) larger than the eyes, position on the face at marked points; fix eyes over these, following manufacturer's instructions. Snip into the large dot at V in head sections. Make an inverted pleat in the ears on the lower raw edges, pin them into the top open edge of the head from the right side

of fabric and machine in position on the wrong side. Close up opening with small stitches on underside. Turn to the right side and stuff the head firmly with the wadding.

Cut the wood to required lengths. Make a hole in the long bar, 40cm (15in) from the top, and wide enough to take the cross bar. Insert cross bar and dab with glue to secure. Screw the knobs into the ends of the cross bar. Dye the wood with mahogany stain and paint on two coats of varnish. Machine a narrow hem around the neck edge of the horse, thread string through and draw up. When varnish is dry, insert the wood into the middle of the horse's neck, secure with glue, adjust the string enclosing the wood, knot string and tuck up loose ends.

To make halter, join two strips of braid to fit round horse's nose, with a brass ring at each side; then attach the fringed braid to the rings to form reins. Sew bells to the fringed braid and then the halter around the horse's nose in the marked position.

Open up the mop head and remove the strings, then cut a 20cm (8in) length of tape and machine the string pieces down the middle of the centre of the tape. Hand-sew the tape vertically down the neck, turning in both ends. Make a half fringe in a similar way and sew onto the head in front of the ears. Trim the ends of the string hair to neaten off.

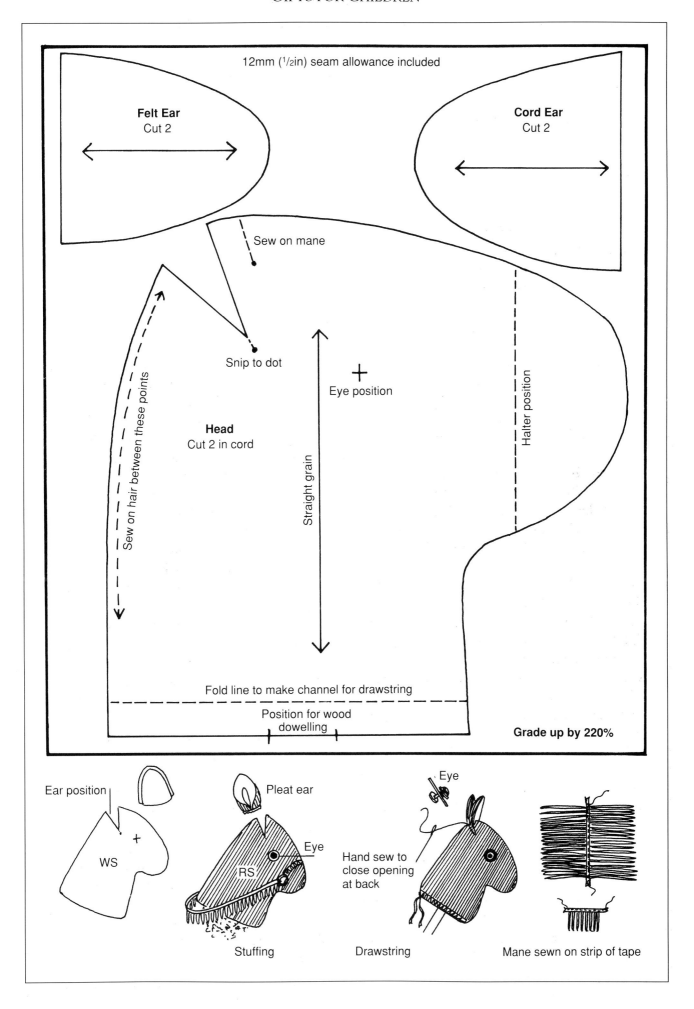

12mm (¹/₂in) seam allowance included

Felt Ear
Cut 2

Cord Ear
Cut 2

Sew on mane

Snip to dot

Sew on hair between these points

+
Eye position

Halter position

Head
Cut 2 in cord

Straight grain

Fold line to make channel for drawstring

Position for wood dowelling

Grade up by 220%

Ear position

WS

Pleat ear

Eye

RS

Stuffing

Eye

Hand sew to close opening at back

Drawstring

Mane sewn on strip of tape

CLOWN CLOTHES HOOK

Not only will this jolly clown brighten up a child's bedroom, but it will double up as a coat hook.

MATERIALS

25cm (10in) square of 6mm (^{1}/4in) multicore plywood
3cm (1^1/4in) diameter wood knob with base
Acrylic paints, brushes
Clear varnish
Fine sandpaper
Tracing paper
Hand fretsaw or Spiralux Electro-Magnetic saw
Hand drill and bit to fit screws
Metal clamps
2 brass screws 2.5 cm (1in) long, 1 brass ring

Grade up and trace the outline of clown's head onto the plywood. Clamp wood to a work bench (to prevent damaging surface you can put a piece of card under the clamp). With one hand on top of the wood, hold fretsaw in other hand and begin sawing towards the outline of the face. Work the saw in an up and down movement, the teeth of the saw horizontal to the edge of the wood. Saw small sections at a time, following the outline as you go. Where there is a sharp angle saw up to the line, then saw in from another point to meet up, enabling a small piece of wood to be removed. Sand the outer edges of the cut pieces. Drill holes in marked spots for the screws.

Trace the features onto the wood and paint in with acrylic paints, starting with the flesh colour for the face. Paint the eyes, mouth, hat and hair; also paint the top of the wood knob red for the nose. When dry, screw the knob onto the face, through the hole from the back. Paint the front and nose with two coats of varnish. When dry the clown is ready to fix to a wall with the remaining screw and brass ring.

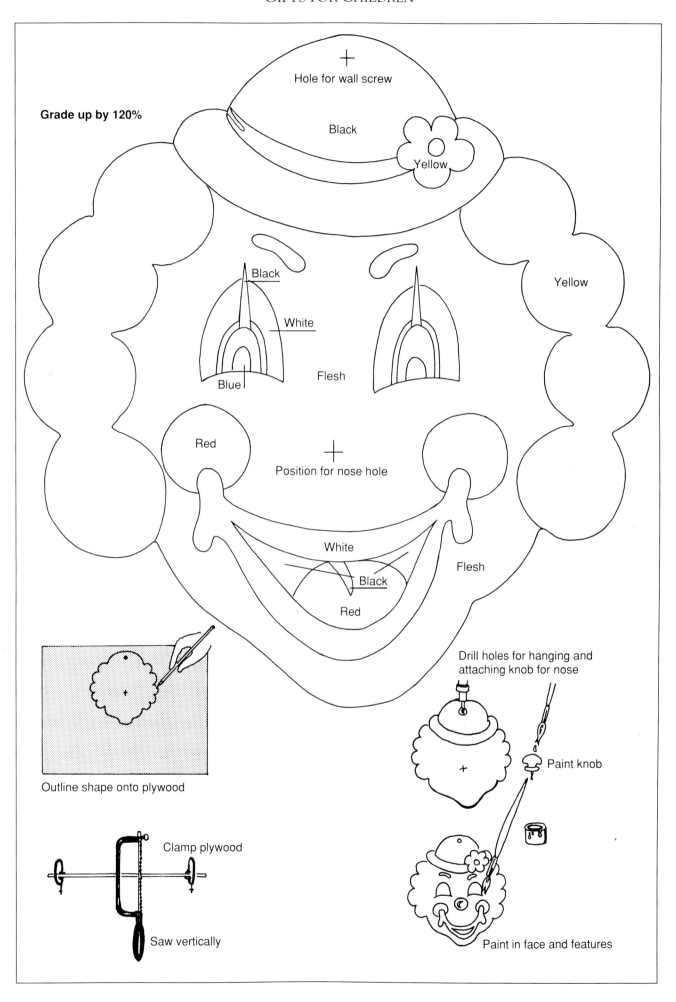

Grade up by 120%

Hole for wall screw

Black

Yellow

Black

White

Blue

Flesh

Yellow

Red

Position for nose hole

White

Black

Flesh

Red

Outline shape onto plywood

Clamp plywood

Saw vertically

Drill holes for hanging and attaching knob for nose

Paint knob

Paint in face and features

SANTA PULL TOY

*T*his amusing little chap will give much pleasure as you can pull his arms and legs up and down, making him dance a jig. He can be made out of thin card and paper holders for a similar effect.

MATERIALS

20cm (8in) square of 6mm (^{1}/4in) multicore plywood
Small wooden bead
Fretsaw, pliers, clamps
Tracing paper
Small screw-in ring for hanging
Four 6mm (^{1}/4in) brass screws
Acrylic paints and brush
1m (40in) strong cotton thread
Drill and bit to fit screws

Trace shapes onto plywood and cut out with fretsaw, following the same method as for the clown on page 114; as each piece is small and in some cases the wood can splinter, some care will be needed!

Fix an arm section in the clamp with the edge uppermost, and drill a hole through to the other side 6mm ($^.3$/4in) from top of arm. Repeat process for other arm and leg pieces. Carefully drill screw hole in marked spots on leg and arm sections.

Paint the clothes, face and other details, remembering to carry the colours over the edges where appropriate. The back can be painted or left natural.

Knot a 25cm (10in) length of cotton through the holes in the leg and arm sections: the knot should be on the outside edge of the limbs as diagram. Snip the points off the ends of the screws with pliers to shorten, screw leg and arm pieces to the back of the body in marked areas. Knot all four lengths of thread together in the middle of the back, and attach wooden bead to these at the bottom, knotting the ends together. Movable toys are best left unvarnished. Fix screw-in ring to the top of the head for hanging up.

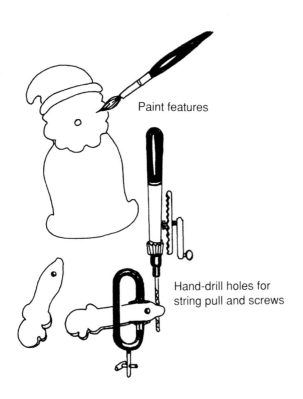

Paint features

Hand-drill holes for string pull and screws

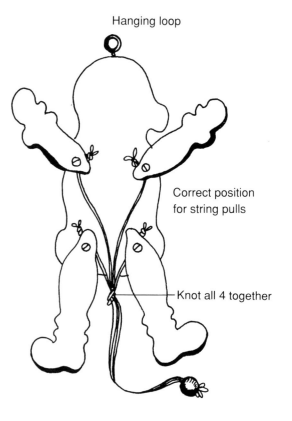

Hanging loop

Correct position for string pulls

Knot all 4 together

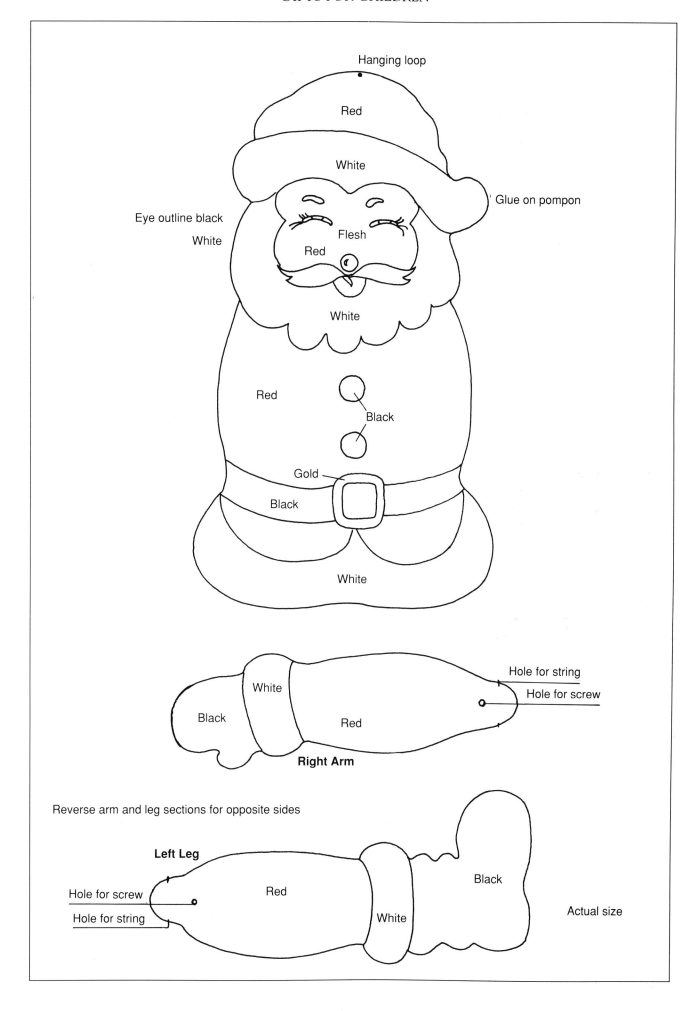

Hanging loop

Red

White

Glue on pompon

Eye outline black

White

Flesh

Red

White

Red

Black

Gold

Black

White

White

Black

Red

Right Arm

Hole for string

Hole for screw

Reverse arm and leg sections for opposite sides

Left Leg

Red

Black

Hole for screw

White

Hole for string

Actual size

PRINCESS BEATRICE

*M*ake this delightful doll for a special little girl: she is sure to be cherished for years to come. Her finished height is 56cm (22in).

MATERIALS

DOLL

50cm (20in) beige cotton 90cm (36in) wide
1 bag polyester wadding
50g (2oz) ball brown double knit yarn
30cm (12in) tape 12mm (¹/2in) wide
Fixative spray
Watercolour paints and brush
Tracing paper, card

CLOTHES

Tartan Dress

70cm (28in) tartan brushed cotton 90cm (36in) wide
1.5m (60in) scalloped-edge lace, 12mm (¹/2in) wide
30cm (12in) scalloped-edge lace, 2.5cm (1in) wide
3 rosebud trims, 2 press-stud fasteners
30cm (12in) elastic 6mm (¹/4in) wide
30cm (12in) tape 12mm (¹/2in) wide
20cm (8in) strip of iron-on interfacing, 2cm (³/4in) wide

Lined Velvet Cape

60cm (24in) velvet 90cm (36in) wide
60cm (24in) lining fabric 90cm (36in) wide
50cm (20in) down feather trim
50cm (20in) velvet ribbon 2cm (³/4in) wide

Silk Pantaloons

30cm (12in) silk satin fabric 90cm (36in) wide
65cm (26in) scalloped-edge lace, 2cm (³/4in) wide
30cm (12in) elastic 6mm (¹/4in) wide
2 ribbon bows

Suede Boots

Scraps of suede
12 hooks and eyes
1 machine needle suitable for leather

DOLL

Grade up the pattern pieces on pp122-4 (see Techniques) and make card templates. Cut out in the beige fabric two head pieces, two body pieces, four leg pieces, two arm pieces on fabric folded in half; ensure that all are cut according to the grain lines. Mark notches for matching up pieces. Machine the leg pieces together on the wrong side taking a 6mm (¹/4in) seam allowance and leaving top open; snip up to the seamline at intervals of 12mm (¹/2in) around curved edges. Turn to the right side and stuff with the wadding up to the knee point. Machine across the middle to make a knee joint on both legs. Finish stuffing to within 6mm (¹/4in) of the top of the leg and tack across opening.

Machine arm pieces on the wrong side, leaving top open, and make a small dart on top arm as marked. Snip seams, turn to right side and wad; make joints in middle of arms as for leg pieces; topstitch fingers on hands where marked.

Pin the raw edges of the legs across the raw edge of the right side of one body piece, legs upturned; machine across. Lay front body piece on back piece with right sides together and machine across the shoulders, leaving the neck open.

Pin the arms from right side of the body section into the side seams at the marked points, thumbs facing inwards. Turn up 6mm (¹/4in) hem at the base of the front piece, machine down the side seams incorporating the arms and across upturned hem. Turn the body to the right side, fill with wadding up to the neck, hem across the base with small stitches.

PRINCESS BEATRICE

Make darts in both head sections, machine the pieces together on the wrong side, snip up to the seam line on curved edges. Turn to the right side, stuff firmly with the wadding, and spray the face with fixative. Copy the features onto the face and paint in. Embroider a face if you wish or use buttons for eyes; all methods have their own charm. Turn up a 6mm (¹/4in) hem at base of head and sew head over neck with small stitches.

To make hair, cut two lengths of tape, one 18cm (7in), one 12cm (5in), and a piece of card 30cm (24in) deep and 16cm (6¹/4in) long. Wrap the wool around the card until well covered. Cut open one edge of the wool and lift off, laying the strands evenly along the centre length of the longer tape; machine down the tape distributing the wool evenly along it as you stitch. Cut 18cm (7in) lengths of wool for the fringe and machine them across the short piece of tape. Sew fringe to front of the head in front of the seamline with small stitches; lay hair on the head running vertically front to back, tucking in both ends of tape. Back-stitch hair to head through all thicknesses, dab some glue to secure hair at sides of head.

DRESS

Grade up the pattern pieces (see Techniques) onto some paper. Cut out in fabric following the instructions on pattern pieces: cut one skirt and two bodices on folded fabric matching fold line on pattern; cut two skirt backs, four bodice backs, two sleeves, two collar pieces. Position one strip of 2.5cm (1in) wide scalloped-edge lace 7.5cm (3in) to the left and one strip to the right, down the centre front of the bodice, and zigzag stitch the two to the front along the straight edges. Sew the bodice fronts to the bodice backs at the shoulder seams, taking 6mm (¹/4in) seam allowance. Press seams open.

Iron interfacing onto reverse of one collar section. Machine sides of the collar on the wrong side of the fabric, turn to right side. Gather 15cm (6in) of the 2.5cm (1in) wide lace to fit the opening at the top collar edge, turn in raw edges, insert lace and machine through all layers. Top-stitch around sides and across top edge of collar. Place the collar between the bodice and lining pieces and machine on the wrong side around the neck edge and back opening edges. Trim seams, snip curves, turn to the right side and press.

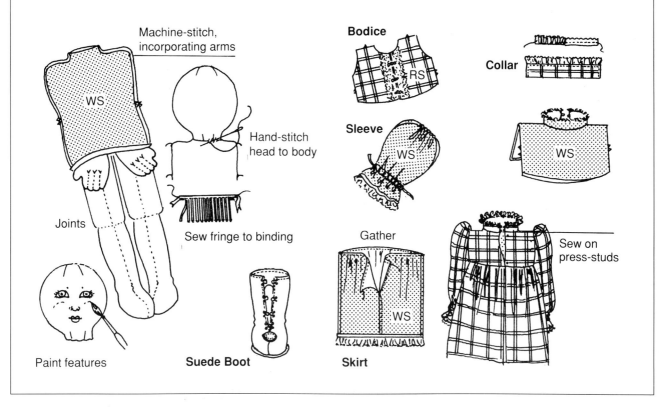

Machine-stitch, incorporating arms

Hand-stitch head to body

Joints

Sew fringe to binding

Paint features

Suede Boot

Bodice

RS

Collar

Sleeve

WS

WS

Gather

WS

Skirt

Sew on press-studs

PRINCESS BEATRICE

Machine 6mm (^{1}/4in) hem on wrong sides of both sleeve edges, machine the narrow lace on top inside hemmed edge. Machine the tape to the wrong side of the sleeve 6cm (2^1/2in) up from the hem, making a channel for the elastic casing, leaving both ends open. Insert the elastic to draw up to fit the wrists of the doll, machine across both ends to secure. Repeat for other sleeve. Run two rows of gathering stitches around each sleeve head, to draw up. Pin sleeve heads to the bodice armhole sections with right sides together, space the gathers evenly and machine in position on the wrong side. Then machine up the sides of the bodice and down the sleeves on the wrong side. Neaten raw edges with zigzag stitch, snip curves around the armhole and turn to the right side and press.

French seam the sides and centre back skirt seam up to marked point (see Techniques). Turn up a 2.5cm (1in) hem on the skirt and machine the narrower lace to the hem on the inside edge. Gather the top of the skirt with two rows of gathering stitches between marked points, draw up to fit the bodice. With skirt fabric on the right side, press under a 12mm (^{1}/2in) turning along the left edge of the back opening. Do the same to the left bodice opening edge. Right sides of fabric together, pin the bodice to the skirt, matching the pressed back opening edges at the waist. Machine the bodice to the skirt, then neaten the raw edges at the waist by zigzag stitching together on the wrong side of the fabric. Stitch press-studs to marked positions on bodice back. Sew on the ribbon roses to the bodice front.

LINED CAPE

Grade up the pattern (see Techniques) onto paper, mark sewing notions and grain lines. Cut cape and hood pieces in velvet and lining fabric. Ensure that the pile of the velvet is cut rough side up (to determine this, stroke up and down the fabric with the palm of your hand; you will feel the rough and smooth way in which the pile runs). With right sides together, machine-stitch the centre back seams in the hood pieces. With two rows of gathering stitches gather both the top edges of the cape and lining sections. Pin top edge of velvet cape to base of hood and right sides of lining together, and machine both edges on wrong side. Pin right sides of lining to right side of velvet cape, insert velvet ribbon ties from the outside at marked points. Machine around outer edges on the wrong side, leaving open between points on lower edge. Trim the seam, snip curves and turn to the right side of fabric. Close up opening with small stitches, press carefully on the wrong side around outer edge. Sew the down trim to the outer edge of the hood.

PANTALOONS

Grade up pattern (see Techniques). Cut out in fabric two fronts and two back pieces. Machine centre fronts and backs together on wrong sides, neaten raw edges with zigzag stitches. Pin the front piece to the back at inner leg edges on wrong side and machine. Hem the leg pieces on the wrong side with a 12mm (^{1}/2in) turning, and sew on lace across hem. Machine side seams together.

Turn down hem of 12mm (^{1}/2in) along the top inside edge of the pants and machine, leaving an opening for inserting the elastic. Thread elastic through, draw up to fit doll's waist and sew ends together. Close opening with small stitches. Sew ribbon bows at centre fronts on lace edge.

BOOTS

Cut four boot uppers, two soles, two tabs and two inner tongues in suede as shown. Machine front seam together up to notch on the wrong side of shoe upper, taking 6mm (^{1}/4in) allowance; turn back the long front edges and machine back on the wrong side.

Place the tongue on the inside of the front opening with narrow edge at the bottom, and lay the small tab on the outside; machine the two together through all thicknesses on the right side. Stitch back seam together on the wrong side, fold the top edges over to the inside and machine down. Stitch the sole to the upper on the right side. Sew the hooks and eyes to the front opening. Repeat above method for the other boot.

PRINCESS BEATRICE

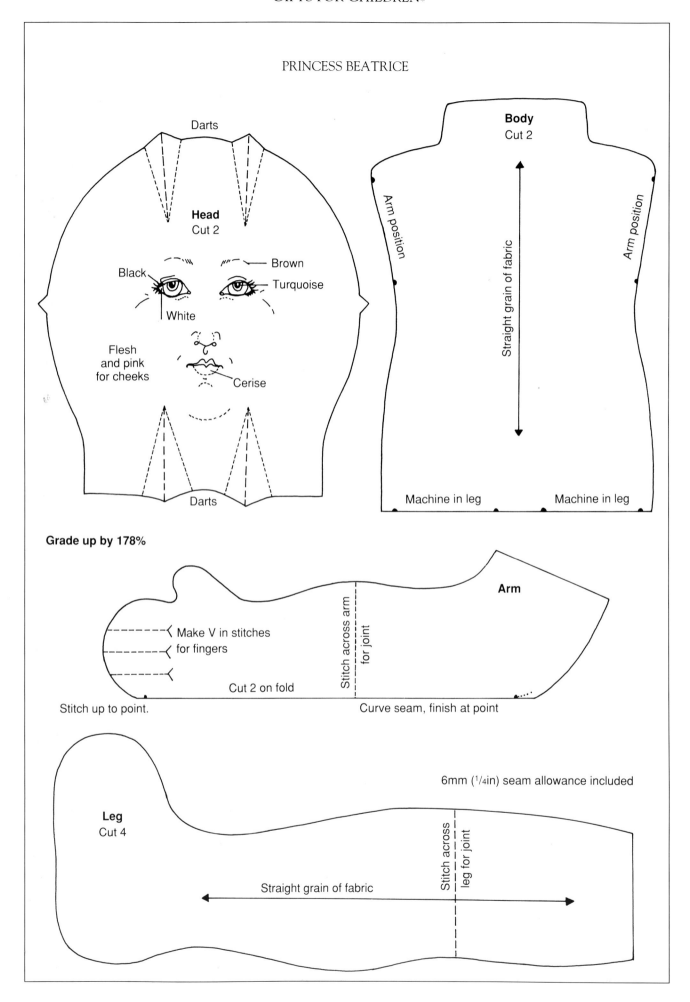

Darts

Head
Cut 2

Black
White
Brown
Turquoise

Flesh
and pink
for cheeks

Cerise

Darts

Body
Cut 2

Arm position

Straight grain of fabric

Arm position

Machine in leg

Machine in leg

Grade up by 178%

Make V in stitches
for fingers

Stitch across arm
for joint

Arm

Cut 2 on fold

Stitch up to point.

Curve seam, finish at point

6mm (¼in) seam allowance included

Leg
Cut 4

Stitch across
leg for joint

Straight grain of fabric

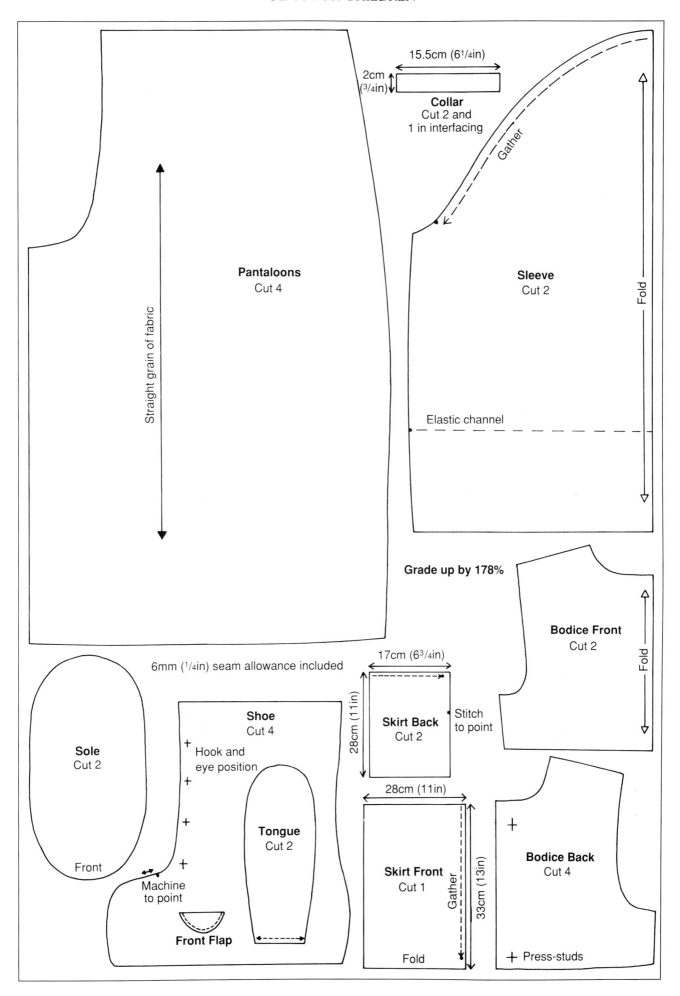

15.5cm (6¼in)

2cm
(¾in)

Collar
Cut 2 and
1 in interfacing

Gather

Sleeve
Cut 2

Fold

Pantaloons
Cut 4

Straight grain of fabric

Elastic channel

Grade up by 178%

Bodice Front
Cut 2

Fold

6mm (¼in) seam allowance included

17cm (6¾in)

28cm (11in)

Skirt Back
Cut 2

Stitch
to point

Sole
Cut 2

Front

Shoe
Cut 4

Hook and
eye position

+
+
+
+

Machine
to point

Tongue
Cut 2

Front Flap

28cm (11in)

Skirt Front
Cut 1

Gather

33cm (13in)

Fold

Bodice Back
Cut 4

+ Press-studs

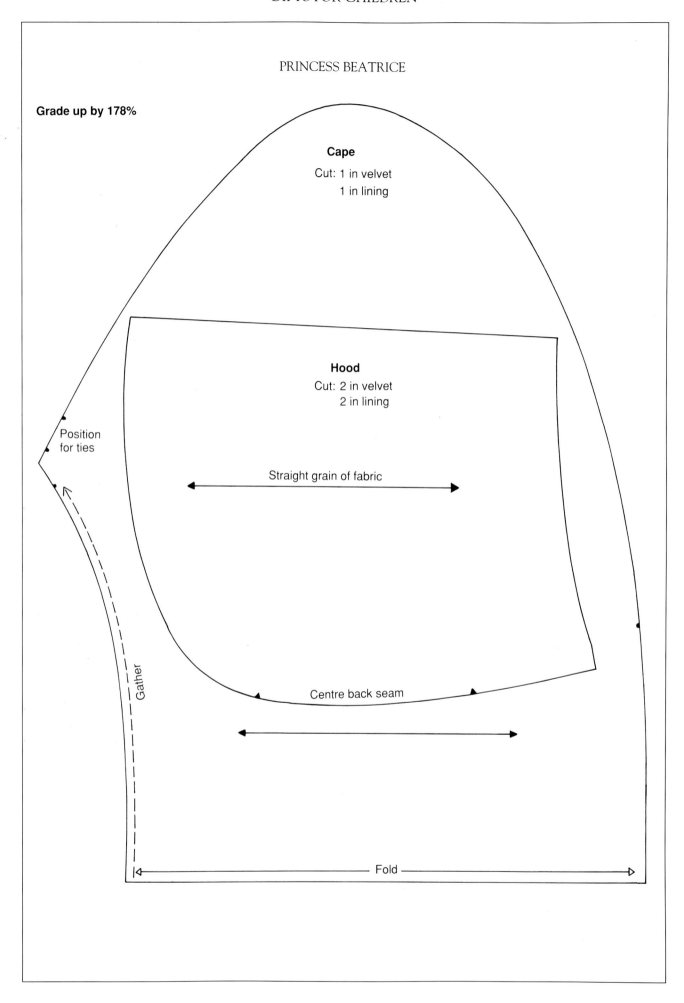

PRINCESS BEATRICE

Grade up by 178%

Cape
Cut: 1 in velvet
1 in lining

Hood
Cut: 2 in velvet
2 in lining

Position for ties

Straight grain of fabric

Gather

Centre back seam

Fold

BABY BIB AND FACE WIPE

*M*ake this delightful bib for baby's first Christmas to join in with the festivities. Change the ribbon and hat colour and you have a lovely gift for a newborn baby.

MATERIALS

Bib with cross-stitch panel
Face flannel
60cm (24in) tartan ribbon 12mm (1/2in) wide
Scraps of cotton fabric: brown, beige, red, white
Iron-on interfacing
2 small black beads
1 pompon (optional)
Tracing paper
Stranded embroidery cotton in the following colours:

	DMC	ANCHOR
Gold	729	874
Red	816	43
Green	904	245
Black	noir	403

Machine the ribbon onto lower edge of bib and 4cm (1½in) up from hem of flannel around edges, turning in the ends. Work cross stitch along the panel insert, following the chart overleaf.

Trace the outline of the face and hat pieces onto the appropriate coloured scraps of fabric. Iron interfacing onto the wrong side; with this side face down, pin the head of teddy in the middle on the front side of the bib. Zigzag or blanket-stitch onto the bib, stitch the hat and mouth pieces on top of the head fabric, trim away excess fabric close to stitching. Sew on the beads for the eyes and make small stitches for the nose, and sew on the pompon securely, if used.

> **SAFETY FIRST**   *Never allow a baby to suck the bib in case the pompon or bead eyes are pulled off and swallowed.*

Baby Bib   Sew on beads for eyes

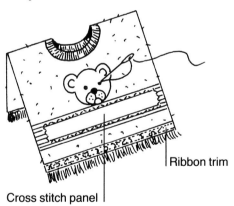

Cross stitch panel   Ribbon trim

Face Wipe

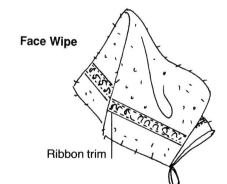

Ribbon trim

Appliqué Teddy for Bib

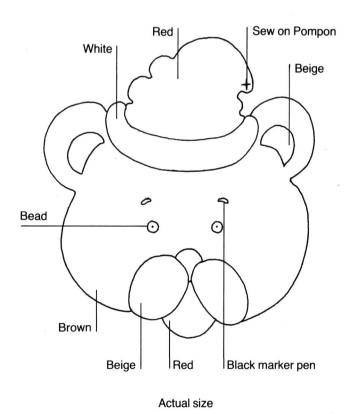

White   Red   Sew on Pompon

Beige

Bead

Brown

Beige   Red   Black marker pen

Actual size

The chart is 112 stitches wide by
32 squares deep

	DMC		ANCHOR
Backstitch	729	——	874
French knot	816	•	43
	816	☒	43
	816	☑	43
	904	⊙	245

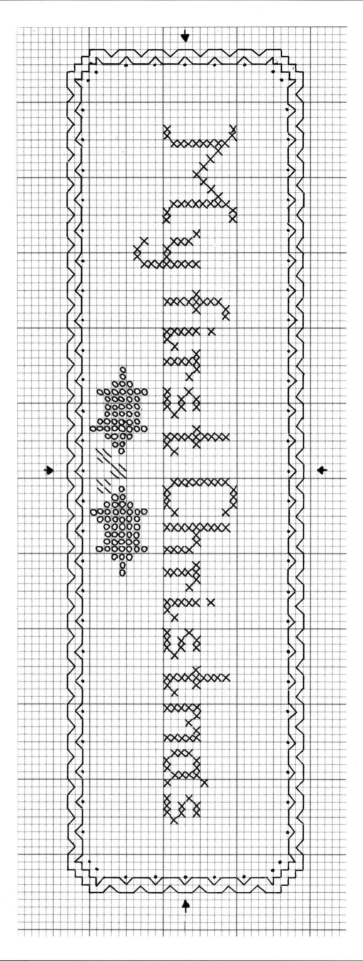

CHRISTMAS TREE

The little Christmas Tree was born
And dwelt in open air;
It did not guess how bright a dress
Some day its boughs would wear;
Brown cones were all, it thought, a tall
And grown-up Fir would bear.

O little Fir! your forest home
Is far and far away;
And here indoors these boughs of yours
With coloured balls are gay,
With candle-light, and tinsel bright,
For this is Christmas Day!

A dolly-fairy stands on top,
Till children sleep; then she
(A live one now!) from bough to bough
Goes gliding silently.
O magic sight, this joyous night!
O laden, sparkling tree!

CHRISTMAS TREE Fairy

MyfirstChristmas

BABY'S CHRISTMAS BOOTEE

Even the tiniest member of the family can have a stocking for Father Christmas to fill when you make this jolly one, or make a pair for baby to wear on Christmas Day.

MATERIALS (TO MAKE A PAIR)

25g (1oz) gold yarn
25g (1oz) white four-ply
50g (2oz) red four-ply
Pair 3¼mm (UK 10, USA 3) needles
Crochet hook, size 1.25mm (UK 3, USA 8)
Pair double-ended 3¼mm (UK 10, USA 3) needles
4 white pompons
Tension: On 3¼mm (UK 10, USA 3), 26 sts and 36 rows in st st make 10cm (4in)
(For knitting terms and methods, see Techniques)

With 3¼mm (UK 10, USA 3) needles and red four-ply yarn, cast on 37 sts and knit into the back of each stitch for first row. Continue in st st for 2.5 cm (1in), ending on a purl row. Start the picot edge as follows: join in gold yarn, K1, * yfwd, K2tog, rep from * to end. Next row purl, break off gold yarn and continue in red, working in st st for 2 rows. Then work rows from chart A, joining in white as required for heart motif; break off white, purl 1 row. Eyelet row: * K2tog, yfwd, repeat from * to last st, K1. Purl 1 row. Following row K to last 11 sts, turn and leave the remaining sts on double-ended needle. Next row purl 15 sts, leaving the remaining 10 sts on other double-ended needle and continue working across the 15 sts for 4 rows in st st; follow 15 rows from chart B for the snowflake design, joining in the white yarn where appropriate. Break off white yarn, purl one row in red yarn and next row decrease 1 st at each end and then on the following two alternate rows until 9 sts remain.

Sock sides: with right side facing pick up and knit 20 sts on left edge of extended piece, knit 11 sts from double-ended needle, turn, purl across 40 sts. Wrong side uppermost pick up 21 sts along other edge of extension and purl 10 sts from double-ended needle (total 72 sts). Continue on these sts in st st for 4 rows, ending on a purl row.

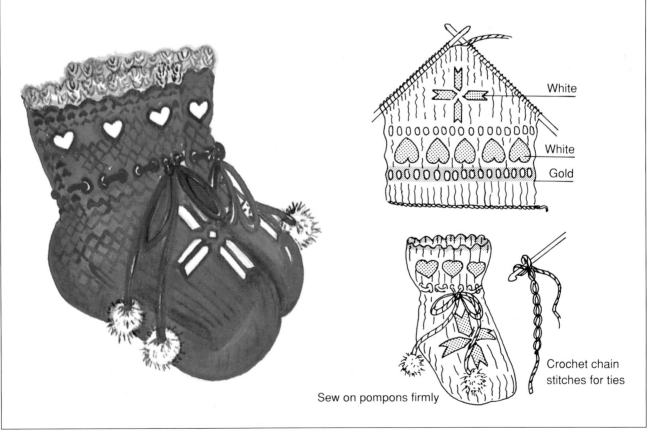

White

White

Gold

Sew on pompons firmly

Crochet chain stitches for ties

BABY'S CHRISTMAS BOOTEE

Following row K42, slp st dec(K), turn and leave last 28 sts on double-ended needle. Next row P13, P2tog, turn and leave remaining sts on double-ended needle.

Work the sole shaping by decreasing 1 st on every row from each of the 28 sts as above method, reducing to 7 on each needle with 14 in the centre, and ending on a purl row. Break off yarn, graft invisibly the remaining sts to last 7 worked sts. Graft remaining 7 central sts to first 7 sts. Sew back seam together on the wrong side, fold the top picot edge to the inside and stitch hem.

Crochet a length of 110 ch sts for tie, thread through the eyelet holes, sew pompons firmly to the ends. Press to finish off.

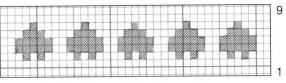

Chart A is 37 stitches wide by 9 rows deep

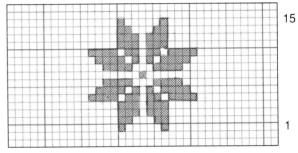

Chart B is 15 stitches wide by 15 rows deep

RABBIT MOBILE

Make the frame as for the cheery Father Christmas mobile on page 26.

MATERIALS

Printed scraps of fabric
4 pompons, 4 ribbon bows
Card, tracing paper
Polyester wadding

Trace the rabbit outline onto card, and cut out two in four different prints. Machine 6mm (¹/4in) from edge around the outline, leaving open between marked points. Snip fabric up to the sewing line at 12mm (¹/2in) intervals. Turn to the right side and gently push the ears and feet out with a blunt point. Stuff with wadding, making sure all areas are well filled. Close up the opening with small stitches. Sew on the tail and bow at marked positions. Sew cotton hanging thread in between the rabbit's ears, and fix to mobile bars.
Reminder: All mobiles should be hung out of reach of babies and young children.

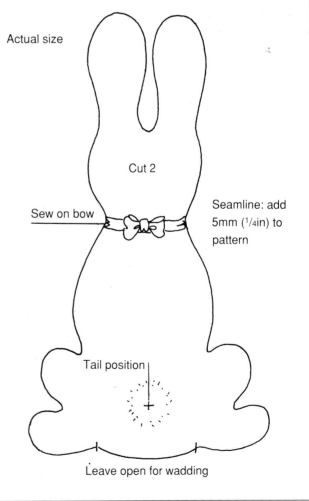

Actual size

Cut 2

Sew on bow

Seamline: add 5mm (¹/4in) to pattern

Tail position

Leave open for wadding

CHAPTER EIGHT

STOCKING FILLERS

FELT STOCKING

Make this stocking as big as you like, just grade up the size for a giant one, and fill with Christmas goodies.

MATERIALS

Felt
Synthetic fur fabric
Tracing paper
Poinsettia flower trim
Glue

Grade up outline on page 45 (see Techniques) and cut out two pieces in felt and two strips of fur fabric 25cm (10in) deep to fit across the top edge of the stocking. Machine a fur strip across each top edge; press the seams up towards the fur fabric.

With right sides of the stocking together machine along the outer edge down the fur fabric and felt, 12mm (1/2in) in. Snip up to the seamline around the curves. Turn stocking to the right side and press, fold the fur in half and press across the fold. Slip-stitch the fur over the seam on the inside of the stocking. Glue on flowers to the fur fabric, or add trim as required. Make one stocking for each member of the family and embroider their initials in chain-stitch·

LAVENDER LADY PEG DOLL

Make this delightful perfumed sachet as a stocking filler, or attach to a fabric-covered box as a decoration.

MATERIALS

Scraps of cotton fabric, lace, felt, ribbon and ribbon roses
Wooden peg (traditional dolly type)
Small saw
Glue
Enamel paints and varnish
Pipe cleaner
Cocktail stick
Lavender seeds
Bead

Cut prongs off peg with a saw, paint the features and hair in enamel paints and varnish when dry. Wrap pipe cleaner around the waist for arms. For sleeves, machine a tube of fabric 3cm (1¹/4in) wide x 8cm (3¹/4in) long, sewing on the wrong side and leaving an opening in the middle. Turn right side out. Make a slit in fold above the opening and insert the head and arms of doll. Glue strips of lace to ends of sleeves.

For the skirt, make a pouch by machining down the sides on reverse of strip of fabric 20cm (8in) long and 8cm (3¹/4in) wide. Fill with lavender, gather up at the top and glue to the torso of peg doll. Glue on lace at hem and around the neckline.

Cut a piece of felt in a petal shape for the hat, mould over the thumb to make crown, sew on ribbon ties at narrow edges and attach to head of doll.

For the parasol cut a quarter-circle of fabric 5cm (2in) deep, glue lace to curved top right side edge, machine straight edges together on wrong side. Turn to right side and insert cocktail stick, pushing through at the pointed end. Gather up and glue top edge of the parasol to the stick, and glue on bead for handle and ribbon rose trim: glue parasol to doll.

Red felt

Paint on features

Lavender-filled sachet

MINIATURE SILHOUETTE IN OVAL FRAME

This would make a lovely gift for a young girl to hang up in her bedroom or for grandmother's sitting room.

MATERIALS

Bakable moulding clay
Card, tracing paper
Flocked paper
Glue
Adhesive picture loop
Black ink and pen
Ribbon 12mm (^{1}/$_2$in) wide
Bronze spray paint

Outline for Silhouette

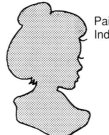

Paint shaded area with Indian ink

Rose Petal

Moulded in clay for frame decoration

Twist two lengths of clay together, enough to join up and form a 6cm (2^1/$_2$in) oval. Make some rosebuds in the clay by moulding petal shapes together, and fix to the top of the oval. Cook in the oven, following manufacturer's details, and spray with bronze paint when cool.

Trace the silhouette onto some paper and fill in with black ink before gluing to the card. Cut some card and flocked paper the size of the oval. Insert the hanging loop from front of the flocked paper to the back. Glue the back of the flocked paper to the back of the silhouette, then glue the frame onto the front of this. Insert the ribbon in the hanging loop, finish off by gluing on a bow.

CHILD'S APPLIQUÉD GLOVES

For a fun pair of gloves, decorate some bought ones with a cheery lion motif.

MATERIALS

1 pair of purchased gloves
2 embroidered cat's-face motifs
Yellow wool, darning needle
20cm (8in) straight white tape 6mm (^{1}/$_4$in) wide

Blanket-stitch around the edges of the gloves in wool (for method see Techniques). Cut 2.5cm (1in) lengths of yellow wool and machine them down the centre of a 10cm (4in) strip of tape. Cut one edge of the wool flush to the tape, neaten up the other edge of the wool, trim if necessary. Pin fringe in a circle around the edge of the motif on the reverse side, forming the lion's mane; stitch in position with small running stitches. Lay and pin the 'lion's head' on the top part of one glove section, turn to the inside of the glove and sew firmly in place. Repeat for other glove.

MODELLED BROOCHES

This fun craft has many possibilities; once you will be able to develop it further, making all sorts of gifts and ideas.

MATERIALS

Bakable moulding clay in assorted colours
Brooch clasps
Glue, varnish
Oven temperature 130°C/275°F, gas mark 1

GARLAND

Roll three thin sausage shapes in green, press together at one end, plait and then join up into a 5cm (2in) circle by trimming the end and closing together. Make five small balls in red and a red bow, press these onto the ring. Bake in oven, following manufacturer's instructions. When cool, glue on the brooch pin, and varnish brooch.

CHRISTMAS TREE

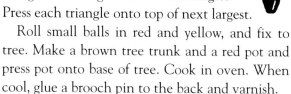

Cut 3 equal-sided triangles in green clay, one 5cm (2in), one 4cm (1½in), one 2.5cm (1in). Snip 12mm (½in) up along bottom edge of all three triangles. Press each triangle onto top of next largest.

Roll small balls in red and yellow, and fix to tree. Make a brown tree trunk and a red pot and press pot onto base of tree. Cook in oven. When cool, glue a brooch pin to the back and varnish.

CHRISTMAS PUDDING

Make a small ball approximately 2.5cm (1in) diameter, flatten in the palm of your hand. Cut some white to imitate icing sugar and press onto the top edge of the pudding. Make three tiny balls in red for holly, two leaves in green, fix to the top of the white clay. Roll a sausage in cream and curve to form a dish to sit the pudding on. Bake in the oven and finish as above.

DECORATED MASK

Make variations of this mask for you and your guests to wear at your Christmas dinner. You could cover the mask with different tapestry fabrics and omit the veiling for the menfolk.

MATERIALS

Bought mask
50cm (20in) scalloped-edge lace 2cm (¾in) wide
Gold spray
Nylon veiling, 13cm (5in) wide
4 gold pipe cleaners
1 bunch gold artificial grapes
Length of wood dowelling as handle
Glue, carpet tape
Ribbon

Spray mask, lace, veiling and wood dowelling gold. Bend the pipe cleaners into coils at one end and join all four together at the other end by twisting around each other. Fold the veiling into two loops, sew the raw edges together and gather up. Glue the lace around the outer edge of the mask on the wrong side, stitch the veiling to the left inside edge. Stitch the bunch of grapes to the outside left edge, and glue the pipe cleaners to the back of them. Glue ribbon around the wood dowelling in a spiral. Glue this to the back left side of the mask and tape in position for added strength. To make the mask more comfortable against the skin, cut some felt to fit on the back. Make holes for eyes and glue this to the mask.

CROSS STITCH KEY RINGS

*M*ake these delightful key rings as an added gift, or use as stocking fillers.

MATERIALS

Bought key rings with embroidery inserts
Scrap of Zweigart Aida fabric 14 holes to
2.5cm (1in)
Stranded embroidery cotton in shades detailed
on key
Tapestry needle size 18
Card

Work cross stitch motif on scrap of canvas, using method from Techniques section and following the charts. Three strands of cotton used throughout. Cut canvas to shape of rings and insert in holder. Cut a piece of card to cover back of work, snap back of frame to close up.

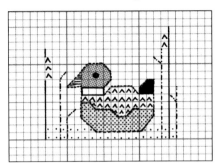

	DMC		ANCHOR
	726	▤	297
	3347	–·–·–	261
Backstitch	310	––––	403
	3064	⬚	347
	986	▦	246
French knot	310	*e*	403
	519	⊡	167
	310	■	403
Blanc	□	1
	300	◪	357

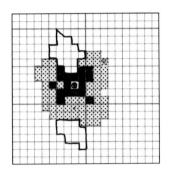

	DMC		ANCHOR
French knot	726	*e*	297
	3608	▨	86
	552	■	100
	986	□	246

HEART-SHAPED PIN CUSHION

*T*his will always come in useful to store those pins and needles that lie around after sewing. Make an extra special one by adding perfumed essence to the filling.

MATERIALS

Scrap of velvet
1m lace 2cm (³/4in) wide
Polyester wadding
Bow trim

Draw heart shape onto card using template from page 45, trace around on a double piece of velvet and cut out, allowing 6mm (¹/4in) seam allowance. Gather up lace with running stitches, then pin lace around the perimeter of one heart piece on the right side with raw edges together and lace facing inwards. Lay other heart piece on top, right side down, then machine around edge 6mm (¹/4in) in, leaving an opening to fill with wadding. Snip up to seam around the curves, turn to right side and stuff. Close up opening with small slip stitches, attach bow at top in centre front.

MATCHING BATH HAT, TISSUE HOLDER AND HANDKERCHIEF

All of these would make welcome gifts for young and old alike. Ring the changes by using pretty pastel floral prints or bright patterns.

MATERIALS

64cm (25in) cotton fabric and lightweight
plastic, 115cm (45in) wide
2.5m (100in) bias binding 12mm (^{1}/2in) wide
2m (80in) lace 3cm (1^1/4in) wide
50cm (20in) elastic 6mm (^{1}/4in) wide
1 packet of handy-size tissues
1 embroidered rosebud flower motif
3 ready-made bow trims

HAT

Cut two circles, one in cotton and one in plastic, 45cm (18in) in diameter. Gather up lace with long machine stitches, and draw up to circumference of outer edge of circle. Lay the fabric circle on top of the plastic one, pin lace around outside edge and machine in place on the right side of the plastic circle. Turn to inside of the plastic circle and pin the bias binding 6cm (2^1/2in) in from outer edge; machine top and bottom edges of the binding to form a casing for the elastic. Leave a small opening for inserting the elastic.

Cut a piece of elastic to fit head measurement, insert into the channel, draw up and secure the ends with small stitches, then close up the opening with small stitches. Stitch a bow to centre front on the lace.

TISSUE HOLDER

Lay packet of tissues on fabric, cut the length of fabric 2.5cm (1in) longer than the packet at both ends. Wrap fabric edges to centre of the packet to gauge the width of fabric: it should meet exactly and not overlap. Cut this oblong in both fabric and plastic. Lay fabric on the plastic, cut binding into strips the same length as narrow edges; pin the binding enclosing long raw edges and

machine. Turn to plastic side, fold bound edges towards the middle and machine across the top and bottom 12mm (^{1}/2in) from the raw edges. Turn to the right side, push out the corner points with a blunt instrument, sew on a bow to each end of the opening. Insert packet of tissues.

HANDKERCHIEF

Cut a square to desired size. Turn up a 6mm (^{1}/4in) hem all the way around the square and machine close to the edge. Press and decorate by sewing on a flower motif or embroidering initials.

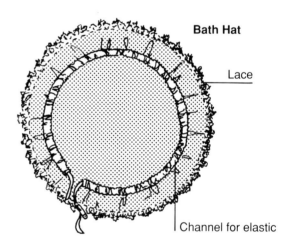

Bath Hat

Lace

Channel for elastic

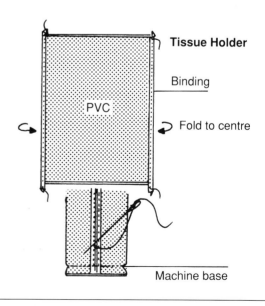

Tissue Holder

Binding

PVC

Fold to centre

Machine base

CHEQUE BOOK COVER

Choose appropriate prints and make a cover for his or her cheque book as an extra little gift.

MATERIALS

1 cheque book for measurements
Card
Print and lining material
Gold lettering
Piping cord, braid
Glue, carpet tape

Cut four pieces of card the length and width of the cheque book. Join two pieces of card together at the short edge with carpet tape, repeat on other two pieces. Cut fabrics to fit the card with a 12mm (^{1}/2in) overlap. Spray glue onto the wrong side of the fabric cover and also onto the wrong side of the lining fabric. Lay one piece of cover fabric onto the card. Snip into the extended fabric piece up to the card edge, to ensure that when folded over fabric lies flat. Press fabric down firmly on the reverse side. Repeat method for card and fabric lining piece.

Glue the gold piping cord trim around the edge of the cover on the wrong side. Cut some braid to fit the width of the card with 6mm (^{1}/4in) overlap at each end; place this on the front of one half of a lining section 4cm (1^1/2in) in from the centre fold. Glue down the overlapping ends to the wrong side at the top and the bottom. Spread glue on the wrong side of the cover section, lay the wrong side of the lining section on top and press down firmly. Put a weighted object on top to ensure both are bonded together well.

Print the words 'Cheque Book' or the person's name on the front cover, using gold adhesive lettering.

DÉCOUPAGE MONEY BOX

Revive the popular Victorian craft of découpage to make these charming gifts, or to revitalise some of your old household items. You can use scraps, or cut-outs from wrapping paper to achieve the same effect.

MATERIALS

Wooden money-box
Black acrylic paint and brush
Clear varnish
Glue
Victorian scrap cut-outs
Fine sandpaper
Sharp scissors

Smooth any rough edges on the box with sandpaper, then paint it all over with the black paint.

Cut out your scraps and work out your design layout; overlap some pieces to add to the effect. Glue the scraps to the box, taking some scraps over the edges and gluing down firmly. Paint over the glued scraps with at least six coats of varnish. After each layer has dried, smooth carefully with fine sandpaper. Eventually the surface will become level.

CHRISTMAS CARD AND GIFT LIST HOLDER

*T*welfth Night and the last of the decorations put away for the next year – save your Christmas cards in this pretty folder. Cover the gift and card records book in co-ordinating fabric and use to log this season's entries.

MATERIALS

Bought card folder and records book
Spray-on fabric glue
1m (40in) velvet ribbon 6mm (1/4in) wide
1m (40in) seasonal printed cotton fabric 90cm (36in) wide for folder
1m (40in) cotton spotted fabric 90cm (36in) wide for book, to co-ordinate with the folder
1 sheet flocked paper, lining paper

Open out the glued edges of the folder. Lay folder out on top of the wrong side of the fabric, outline the shape onto the fabric allowing 2.5cm (1in) for turnings. Spray the fabric on the wrong side with the glue and lay the folder on top. Mitre the ends of the overlaps at the corners and press down edges firmly.

Cut the flocked paper to fit the inside of the folder flush to the edges, spray glue on the reverse and glue to the inside of the folder. Glue the sides of the folder back together. Finally, glue the ribbon around the folder in the middle making a tie at the front.

Cover the records book in the same fashion as the Album on page 103.

NOUGHTS AND CROSSES GAME

*M*ake this quick present to amuse children over the Christmas period. It would also be an excellent game to take on a journey.

Machine the strips of ric rac across and down to form nine equal boxes on the felt, then machine a strip all the way around the outer edge to neaten. Cut out five 'O' and five 'X' shapes in felt.

MATERIALS

25cm (10in) square of red felt
Scraps of black and white felt
1.5m (60in) white ric rac

TECHNIQUES

SEWING AND EMBROIDERY

French Knot
Wrap yarn around the needle tightly before inserting needle back into fabric at start of stitch

Stem Stitch
Draw needle through fabric and over yarn pulling yarn up and back – repeat close to last stitch worked along a line

Buttonhole/Blanket Stitch
Insert needle into fabric, making a small stitch Wrap yarn under needle and draw through fabric

French Seam
Machine edges together close to raw edge on right side. Clip fabric close to seamline Turn to wrong side Press seam. Machine 6mm (¹/₄in) in from seam

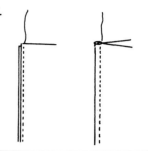

Running/Gathering Stitch
Space stitches equally by pulling needle and yarn up and down through fabric

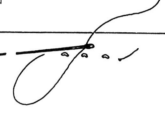

CROCHET

Basic Chain Stitches
1 Make a slip loop by lifting long-end across short and pull through with hook
2 Catch yarn over fingers and pull through loop on hooks

Slip Stitch
Draw hook from front to back through loop of first chain
Pull yarn through loop on hook

Double Crochet
1 Insert hook into 2nd chain from hook
Draw yarn through both loops on hook
2 Next row:
Make 2 chains
Miss double crochet below
Insert hook under 2 loops at top of stitch
Yarn round hook
Draw through 2 loops on hook

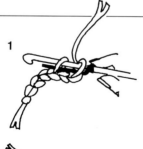

Half Treble
Yarn around hook
Insert hook through top of 3rd stitch below
Yarn around hook
Draw through 3 loops on hook

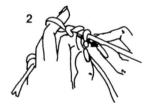
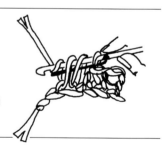

Treble
Wrap yarn around hook once
Insert hook in top loop of 4th stitch left of hook
Yarn around hook
Draw through stitch, giving 3 loops on hook
Yarn around and draw through 2 loops on hook
With 2 loops on hook, draw yarn around hook and through them

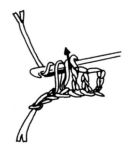

KNITTING

Casting On
1 Make a loop on left needle
Insert right needle through loop
2 Bring yarn up and over right needle
3 Draw loop through and transfer to left needle
Continue for required number of stitches

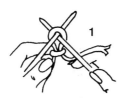

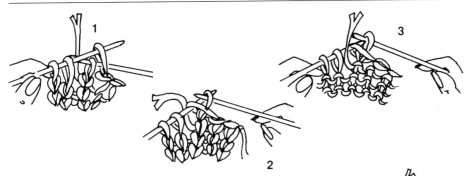

Casting Off
1 Knitwise: Knit 2 stitches
Insert left needle into first stitch
2 Purlwise: Lift first stitch over second and lift off
Repeat across work
3 Purlwise: Purl 2 stitches
Lift right stitch over 2nd purled stitch.
Repeat across row

Knit Stitch
1 Insert needle through front to back of stitch on left needle
2 Draw yarn around and over right needle
3 Draw loop through and lift off to right needle

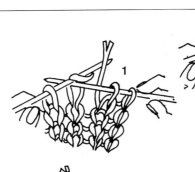
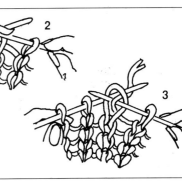

Purl Stitch
1 Yarn on front of work
Insert right needle from back to front of stitch on left needle
2 Draw yarn round right needle
3 Draw yarn through to make new stitch and transfer to right needle

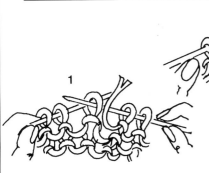

Slip-Stitch Decrease
1 Slip stitch from left to right needle
2 Knit next stitch on left needle
3 Using needle point, lift last knitted stitch over stitch slipped on right needle

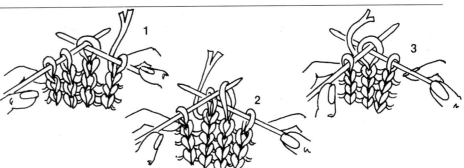

NEEDLEPOINT AND CROSS STITCH

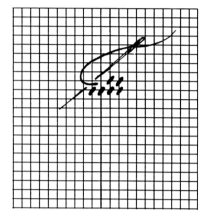

Tent Stitch
Work a diagonal stitch over one
intersection of canvas

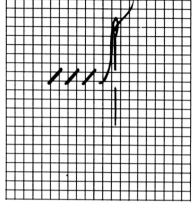

Half Cross Stitch
Work under stitch as diagram from
left to right over 1 block on
Aida/Hardanger fabric

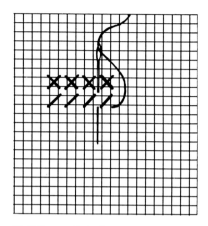

Full Cross Stitch
Work row of half cross stitches
Cross back over worked stitches
from right to left – this ensures
crosses lie in same direction

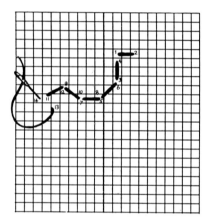

Back Stitch
Use for outlining worked cross
stitch
Insert needle from back of work to
front at 1, down at 2, up at 3, down
at 4 and so on as required

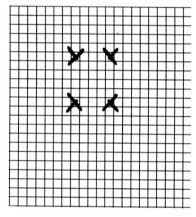

Three Quarter Stitch
Work first half of stitch as full cross
stitch
Cross over stitch comes across and
over worked stitch into *central* hole

GRADING UP PATTERNS

Due to the limitations of page
size, it has not been possible
to reproduce all the patterns
in this book to their original
size. Whenever a pattern
requires grading up, you will
find this marked on the
pattern itself as 'Grade up by
X%'. By far the easiest
method is to take the book
along to your local print or
stationery shop and ask for
the pattern to be photocopied
up to the percentage
specified.

Pompon

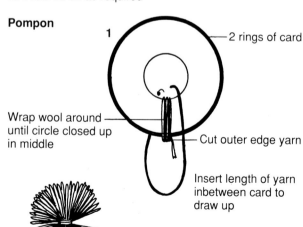

1   2 rings of card

Wrap wool around
until circle closed up
in middle

Cut outer edge yarn

Insert length of yarn
inbetween card to
draw up

2 Draw up yarn to make
pompon. Trim ends

Tassels
1   Cut ends of wool between card

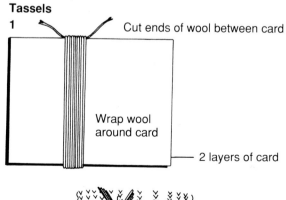

Wrap wool
around card

2 layers of card

2 Insert wool
through
edge of knitting

Pull 2 ends through loop